"Greg Stier takes hi
Gospelize Your You
Greg's commitmen
inside out,' especially as lived in and through teenagers, is what drives his
ministry and grounds this helpful and detailed resource. What he makes
clear from the first pages is that evangelism is not simply a programmatic
option among many for youth ministry, but is rather the core reason and
outcome of a healthy ministry. In *Gospelize Your Youth Ministry*, Greg Stier
provides the foundation, the plan, and the structure to ensure that the book
of Acts lives on in and through your ministry."

Chap Clark, PhD
Editor and contributor, *Youth Ministry in the 21st Century: 5 Views*
Professor of Youth, Family, and Culture, Fuller Theological Seminary

"With *Gospelize Your Youth Ministry* Greg Stier has written a powerhouse
book that, I'm convinced, can transform the way youth ministry is done
in America (and maybe even across the world)! Based on timeless truths
in the book of Acts and the latest evangelism research, this dynamic book
unpacks principles that can transform any youth ministry from typical to
transformational, from meeting driven to mission driven, from entertainment
based to Gospel Advancing. I pray that you and your youth ministry team
take the time to read this book slowly, unpack these principles thoughtfully
and apply these truths passionately. If you do, both you and your youth
ministry will forever be changed."

Josh McDowell
Author, Speaker, Founder of Josh McDowell Ministry, a division of Cru

"I've given my life and ministry to the study of movements, in particular
gospel movements. My friend, Greg Stier, gets movements better than most.
Born in a movement, catalyst in others, and a student of gospel advancement,
reading Greg's book, *Gospelize*, is like drinking from a cool mountain stream
after climbing a '14'er' like he talks about in the book. This book inspires,
and we could use some gospel vision in the church today. But it does more:
it equips, and it gives scores of examples of gospelicious movements in our
time. Your student ministry needs this book. No, your whole church needs it.
Actually, we all do. Read it and be changed. And, advance the gospel!"

Alvin L. Reid, PhD
Professor of Evangelism and Student Ministry/Bailey Smith Chair of
Evangelism, Southeastern Baptist Theological Seminary

"Here's the thing. Too many youth ministry practices function comfortably without Jesus' interference. A 'gospelized' youth ministry risks everything on the premise that Jesus still shows up with love, truth and power when we're faithful. If you're called by Jesus to work with kids, this book will urge you to get reacquainted with Jesus' values for ministry, fix some broken patterns, quit messing around and join the Greatest Multiplication Strategy the world has ever seen. All for Jesus' glory!!"

Dave Rahn
Senior Vice-President, Youth for Christ/USA

"If we don't make disciples, we've MISSED the assignment! Greg's new resource, *Gospelize Your Youth Ministry*, will inspire you to follow your good intentions and to LIVE OUT a deep commitment to making the gospel core to who you are and how you lead your youth ministry. Thank you, Greg, for sharing these practical 'how to's' and especially for being the most gospelized kingdom dude I know!"

Dr. Larry Acosta
Founder and CEO, Urban Youth Workers Institute

"*Gospelize Your Youth Ministry* comes from a heart, mind and life that understands the impact of evangelism on students like no one else. It is an indispensable read for anyone who aspires to have an impact in their youth ministry context. This book is rooted in the Scripture, practical in its application and balanced between the call for students to both 'BE' and 'DO' in their Christian life. Applying the principles of this book will revolutionize your youth ministry and could, in fact, focus the direction of student ministry for years to come."

Kevin Turner, PhD
Professor of Youth Ministry and Theology, Colorado Christian University

"Stier's *Gospelize Your Youth Ministry* not only equips me, but inspires me to share my faith and live out the gospel message like the early believers did in the book of Acts."

Jonathan McKee
Author of *Ministry by Teenagers* and *Real Conversations*

"Practical…biblical…inspirational…and very challenging! I'd highly encourage any leader to interact with *Gospelize Your Youth Ministry*. You will gain new insight into biblical texts and practical strategies to move your ministry forward exponentially."

Dann Spader
Founder, Sonlife and Global Youth Initiative

GOSPELIZE

YOUR YOUTH MINISTRY

A SPICY "NEW" PHILOSOPHY OF YOUTH MINISTRY (THAT'S 2,000 YEARS OLD)

GREG STIER

DARE 2 SHARE

Dedication

To Jonathan Smith,
who went to be with the Lord
on July 12, 2015.
His passion for God,
love of His Word,
and example of humility
made a life-changing impact on me
and countless others.

TABLE OF CONTENTS

FOREWORD

"Believe it or not evangelism is the one biblical purpose that, for the most part, we suck at. Most of us want to believe we're passionate about evangelism, but if we are being honest we'd admit we're unsure how to do it in a way that's natural and effective...and because of that, we remain frustrated. I've invited Greg to help us not suck at evangelism."

That's how I first introduced Greg Stier to a room filled with hundreds of youth pastors.

A few of those pastors were more concerned over my choice of word ("suck") than the fact that they were developing a bunch of teenagers who had no clue or passion for evangelism. Unfortunately, a similar mindset exists amongst youth leaders today—we're often concerning ourselves over the wrong issues.

A decade ago, I wrote the book *Purpose Driven Youth Ministry* in an attempt to help leaders figure out how to balance the biblical purposes of (1) evangelism, (2) fellowship, (3) discipleship, (4) ministry and (5) worship. It was my life's work—my magnum opus if you will. I've taught this material all over the world as the book has been translated into dozens of languages. Here's what's interesting to me, everywhere I speak about God's purposes, regardless of the language and culture, the statement and questions are always the same.

Statement: "We do pretty good at four of the five biblical purposes, but we're terrible at *evangelism.*"

Question: "How do we empower teenagers to care enough about their relationship with Jesus to share Him with others?"

Now, as a result of this book you're holding, there is a thoughtful, biblical, practical, empowering and hopeful answer. It's right here! My prayer is that it will send shockwaves throughout the youth ministry world and change the landscape of evangelism in youth ministry.

Let me be forthright and admit that I'm a big Greg Stier fan. Honestly, if he would have written an "average" book I would still tell people to read his stuff because he's just a good dude. He's an amazing communicator, he's super smart, he's really, really funny, he's one of the most passionate people I know, and he's just a great hang. But, this isn't just an average book...it's an excellent book! It's the clearest articulation I've ever read of how evangelism meets youth ministry. Which means I'll promote it everywhere I go.

Gospelize is Greg's magnum opus.

This book is the culmination of a life lived in pursuit of helping youth leaders mobilize teenagers to care for those who don't know Jesus. If you study it, think deeply about, translate it with your current church culture in mind, it has the potential to change you and your youth ministry.

Greg's ideas don't come from random stories of exceptionally evangelistic youth leaders, instead he frames everything on the timeless values discovered in the Book of Acts. On every page you can feel Greg's heart beating to live out these truths personally and help youth leaders embody them practically.

As I read the pages of this book I was reminded of why I felt God's call into youth ministry so many years ago...because down deep inside, I truly believe that the Good News of Jesus can genuinely heal a broken generation with lasting hope. I've seen it play too many times in different youth ministry situations not to believe that a teenager's life can be totally redirected as a result of Jesus. I'm guessing you believe the same to be true and that's why you're even [at least] slightly interested to better understand youth ministry and evangelism.

Trust me, this book will refresh you, encourage you, and re-focus you on the original Jesus mission that got you into ministry. In addition, it will help you develop a plan of action that will transform the way you view and do youth ministry for the rest of your life. As you learn more about *evangelism,* I encourage you to think deeply about how evangelism connects with the other biblical purposes—it can deepen your *discipleship* efforts, ignite your *ministry* opportunities and enhance your *fellowship.* Apply these ideas with love, humility and consistency and you'll find yourself and your teenagers engaging more fully in *worship.* God's purposes are waiting to be lived-out in you and the youth ministry He has entrusted to you.

Let's stop sucking at evangelism.

Thanks, Greg, for helping us do just that!

Doug Fields
Youth Pastor of 30+ years
Author of 50+ books
Co-founder of Downloadyouthministry.com

INTRODUCTION

I am the result of a Gospel Advancing Ministry.

The church that reached me and my entire family for Christ was a rare breed, indeed. It had a passionate, purposeful focus on reaching teenagers with the gospel. As a result, thousands—that's right, thousands—of teenagers across the Denver metropolitan area were transformed by the good news of Jesus.

Although Colorado Bible Church typically only had a few hundred adults attending on the average Sunday morning, at one point, it had over 800 teenagers in the youth group! Our group was called "Christian Youth Ranch." While this strange moniker might sound more like a home for troubled teenagers, it was instead a vibrant, focused, massive sea of newly believing teenagers who had been radically transformed by the power of the gospel.

Ralph "Yankee" Arnold was the ring leader of this exciting gospel advancing circus. Technically, he was a church planter and a pastor, but down deep inside, he was just a youth leader in Senior Pastor clothing.

He'd initially come to Denver to reach teenagers for Jesus, and found that he had to start a church in order to fund his endeavor. So that's exactly what he did.

Yankee's daddy was a counterfeiter from the backwoods of Georgia who'd headed to the North when he was on the run from the law. When his baby boy was born in a Northern state, the father nicknamed the boy D*@# Yankee.

We just called him Yankee.

When he planted this church and started this youth ministry, it felt like an anomaly. Here was this Southern-twanged preacher nicknamed "Yankee" with the swagger of an Elvis and the charisma of a Clooney, who planted his flag in the Denver suburb of Arvada. With his King James Version of the old *Scofield Reference Bible* and his passion for teenagers, he was ready to reach the city for Jesus— or die trying.

And he certainly could have.

Yankee would do anything to reach teenagers—and I mean anything. I remember once he challenged the teenagers to bring their friends out to youth group, and if they did, he would run "The Egg Gamut." Yankee bought hundreds and hundreds of eggs, dressed himself up in thick clothing and armed a 100-yard long line of teenagers with all the eggs they could throw. When the whistle blew, Yankee ran the gamut from one end of the line to the other as teenagers threw the painful projectiles right at him. He looked like a smashed and mashed omelet mix, complete with egg shells stirred in, by the time he reached the end of the line.

But he didn't care. Teenagers were there. They'd all go into the church auditorium and sing for a bit while he cleaned up. Then Yankee would come out and share the good news of Jesus with the crowd and give them an opportunity to say "yes" to Jesus.

Sometimes it was 100-foot banana split night. Other times, it was a movie night. That's where I first saw *A Thief in the Night*—for those of you old enough to remember this so-bad-it's-good rapture movie. It was fun. And it was focused on one thing... gospel advancement.

And Yankee took the gospel beyond Arvada. He reached into North Denver, where my rough-and-tumble family members ruled the streets. You see, I don't come from a typical, pasty-white, church-going, hymn-singing, Bible-reading family. I come from a family full of body-building, tobacco-chewing, beer-drinking thugs (and that's just the women)!

Seriously, three of my five uncles were bodybuilders, the fourth one was a power lifter who could bench press 500 pounds and the fifth one was a Golden Gloves boxer. All of them could fight. And most of them enjoyed it.

The Denver version of the mafia knew my uncles as "The Crazy Brothers." So when the mafia thinks your family is dysfunctional, that's bad news. And the baddest of the bad was my Uncle Jack.

Jack was ripped. His large biceps were covered in tattoos, like his cheeks were covered by his lamb chop sideburns. Jack had been in and out of jail for all sorts of violent acts, once for choking two cops.

Jack resisted arrest.

Jack resisted everything.

Until one day Yankee came into the picture and dared to reach into a rough, tough part of the city in order to engage in a gospel conversation with Jack. One of Jack's friends, Bob Daly, had been going to Colorado Bible Church. Bob wanted Jack and his family to hear about Jesus, but he was too afraid to share the gospel with such a scary character. So he dared Yankee to do it.

Jack was scary tough, but Yankee was scary bold.

Yankee took the dare and won. After clearly presenting the gospel to Jack in a way that was understandable to him for the first time in his life, Yankee asked Jack if that made sense and if he wanted to trust in Jesus. All Jack could say was, "Hell, yeah!"

Now *that's* a sinner's prayer!

It didn't take long for Jack to start spreading the news. The next day he shared the good news with "Thumper," an Italian bodybuilder he worked with and worked out with. Thumper brought Jack to his house and made him tell his entire family about the message of grace—brothers, sisters, mother, dad—and all of them embraced Jesus' free gift of grace.

I watched in awe as this message transformed Uncle Jack, Uncle Bob, Uncle Tommy, Uncle Dave and eventually, my own mother— the only sister in the group! And finally, after years of praying and pleading, even my ultra-resistant Uncle Richard said, "Hell, yeah!" to Jesus too.

As each one of my family members put their faith in Jesus, Yankee would bring them into the church, train them to share their faith and teach them to grow in Christ. Making disciples who made disciples was as natural to him as breathing. He lived it. He preached it. He programmed it. He chose leaders who modeled it.

Eventually, I became one of those leaders. Although I was only a teenager, I was put in charge of taking other teenagers out on Friday nights to share their faith. I was also given responsibility for my own bus route, which involved going door-to-door on Saturdays, encouraging parents to let us take their children on a bus to Sunday school the next day.

Core to Yankee's strategy was getting as many teenagers as possible to spread the gospel to anyone and everyone.

Yankee trained us to do just that. We had to memorize seven sentences that clearly explained the good news, so that we could explain it to anyone, anywhere, anytime. We were equipped to use illustrations, opening questions and closing questions. We role-played talking to atheists, agnostics, Jehovah's Witnesses, Mormons and you-name-it, so that we were ready for anything and everything.

It worked. By the time I was in my early teen years, I could navigate just about any gospel conversation with any age group.

Because I was relentlessly inspired and equipped in faith sharing essentials, I could talk about Jesus naturally with both friends and strangers. As a result, I was able to reach my next door friend, Mike, for Jesus…and his two brothers…and Benji down the street…and

Carl and Renee across the street. I also had the privilege of leading Vince to Jesus, who then led Rodney to Jesus.

This all happened before I was in the 10th grade.

And I wasn't that "one-of-a-kind" teenager, like you may be thinking. There was an entire core group of teenagers, many from the inner city just like me, who were transformed by the message and mission of Jesus. I think of Tim, who taught me to share my faith, and his brother Kenny, who taught me to preach. There were three sisters, Brenda, Cathy and Patty, all of whom shared Jesus and made disciples. I could go on and on...Rick, Scott, Art, Rich, Manual, Steve, Shelly, Teri, Kim, on and on and on and on...we were all advancing the good news effectively, long before we graduated from high school.

It was this causal—not to be confused with "casual"—form of Christianity that attracted us and kept us engaged. Yankee had given us a mission and a message. We had a camaraderie that went beyond sitting together in a youth room. We were in a foxhole together, waging war against Satan for the souls of our fellow teenagers, and it unleashed us to passionately live and give our faith long after we graduated and scattered.

And it all started with one hillbilly pastor who played the banjo, did the hambone (YouTube it) and was focused on using teenagers to reach teenagers with Jesus' message of grace and hope.

Actually, it didn't start there at all. It actually all started 2,000 years ago, when Jesus unleashed His disciples to "make disciples of all nations."

Yankee just happened to be a follower of Christ who took that commission from Jesus seriously.

And he is not alone.

There are hundreds of youth leaders across North America and beyond today who are implementing these same ancient values that are embedded in the New Testament. They are experiencing explosive spiritual and numeric growth as a result.

You can join the ranks of this causal, missional, Gospel Advancing Movement! You **should** join the ranks, because there is a better way to do youth ministry than what is happening in the typical youth room today. In the coming chapters, I'll be laying out a picture of what building a Gospel Advancing Youth Ministry looks like.

Reading this book is the easy part. Implementing the biblical values in this book is the exciting and challenging part.

But if you're willing to take this journey, you will be re-energized in your youth ministry passion. You will witness your students growing deeper in their relationship with Jesus, as they bring more teenagers into the kingdom.

A fully "gospelized" youth ministry will make every late night text from a struggling teenager, every painfully long church staff meeting and every "the pastor would like to see you now" pop-in from the church secretary because of the dodge-ball-game-gone-bad in the church auditorium well worth it.

Youth ministry is worth it, **if** you're willing to do it right. And there's no better template than how Jesus worked through the early disciples to build His church in the Gospels (Matthew 16:19) and throughout the book of Acts.

Let's start there.

CHAPTER 01

DON'T JUST STAND THERE... GOSPELIZE!

> "But you will receive power when the Holy Spirit comes on you; and you will be my witnesses in Jerusalem, and in all Judea and Samaria, and to the ends of the earth."
>
> After he [Jesus] said this, he was taken up before their very eyes, and a cloud hid him from their sight.
>
> They were looking intently up into the sky as he was going, when suddenly two men dressed in white stood beside them. "Men of Galilee," they said, "why do you stand here looking into the sky? This same Jesus, who has been taken from you into heaven, will come back in the same way you have seen him go into heaven." —Acts 1:8-11

Imagine that moment when Jesus gave His disciples the final charge to go into the world and spread the good news to everyone everywhere. You had just spent the last 40 days reveling in the shocking joy of Jesus' resurrection from a horrific death, and now His pierced, beautiful feet are leaving the ground. Jesus starts floating upward, upward, upward. He goes higher and higher, finally disappearing into the gentle clouds that waft across the deep blue Judean sky.

Then a voice beside you awakens you from what feels like a dream. You turn to see two men dressed in white who've appeared out of nowhere. "Why do you stand here looking into the sky?" they ask. Their pointed question reminds you that Jesus has already given you the mission, the plan and the deadline. They are telling you, in essence, "Don't just stand there...gospelize!"

It started in Jerusalem, and then stretched across Judea. It eventually spread to Samaria and Antioch, then on to Greece and Italy. Over the centuries, Jesus' message and mission have crisscrossed the globe as more and more Jesus followers have embraced the call to do more than just stand there.

As followers of Christ, we have inherited that two millennia old message and mission. Until our Savior returns to planet earth on a cloud, we must be busy with the quest He has called us to accomplish.

The quest to make disciples.

The quest to spread the good news.

The quest to *gospelize.*

TRANSFORMATION FROM THE INSIDE OUT

I love that word "gospelize." I first heard it while I was working out in my basement a few years ago. To be honest, I had purchased one of those infomercial workout DVD series and got tired of listening to the trainer's corny jokes at 6:00 in the morning! So I turned down the sound on the DVD and turned up the sound on my computer. What was I listening to when I heard the word for the first time? Someone reading a 100-something-year-old Charles Spurgeon sermon online. (Yes, I'm a theology nerd!)

Here's what Spurgeon said:

> I contend for this, that to gospelize a man is the greatest miracle in the world. All the other miracles are wrapped up in this one. To gospelize a man, or, in other words, to convert him, is a greater work than to open the eyes of the blind.[1]

Spurgeon didn't invent this word. It was an old English word that simply meant to "evangelize" someone.

Instantly, I was hooked. The word evangelism smacks of bullhorns and pointy fingers of judgment. But gospelize sounds like transformation from the inside out. And, as you well know, this is exactly what this culture of teenagers needs.

From self-harm, to suicide, to self-image challenges, to sexual temptation, this generation has been bombarded by the Evil One. Our young people live in the midst of a generation of walking wounded who are longing for hope and looking for answers.

And Jesus offers them both—and more!

But we are the vehicles that Jesus works through to download this good news to these teenagers. We are His hands, His feet and His mouth. So we must reach out, walk toward and speak up.

Just what does it mean to "gospelize" your youth ministry?

To gospelize your youth ministry is to build a context in which the good news of Jesus is moving both deeply *into* the souls of your teenagers, and outwardly *through* your teenagers to others. When you make the gospel central to everything you are doing, you are gospelizing your ministry.

Gospelizing your youth group is much, much more than simply getting your teenager to share the gospel with their peers. When you read through the book of Acts, evangelism was front and center. But the priority of evangelism wasn't flying solo. The gospel-sharing efforts of the early followers of Jesus sprang out of a context of believers who loved God and loved others. Prayer was a huge emphasis, and so was a commitment to His Word. Converts were not just made, disciples were multiplied. These priorities, plus a few others, became the building blocks that formed the foundation of an ongoing advancement of the good news.

This forward movement of the life-changing message of Jesus was not primarily accomplished through techniques, strategies or methodologies, but in the moving of the Spirit's power, first of all in the early disciples, and then through them to reach others.

So how do you create a context in which this happens on a consistent basis? Ahh, that's what this book is about!

In Acts 1:8, Jesus called His disciples to pursue His mission by being His witnesses, starting where they were at and expanding outward. But led by the Spirit, they didn't just make disciples, they multiplied them! This means life-on-life investment in those who had put their faith in Jesus, and implies training them to reach their spheres of influence. By the time you get to Acts 28 at the end of the book, you see that the gospel had advanced all the way to Rome. The result? Radical gospel transformation both inward and outward!

If you read the book of Acts closely, you can see this was an exciting, messy and dangerous process. But you also see the disciples learning and growing in their ability to advance the gospel, not just personally, but also through other believers.

THE RIGHT STUFF

The book of Acts provides a vibrant picture of what it looks like to gospelize our ministry efforts. Acts not only describes the kind of transformational impact we should be purposefully pursuing, it also points us toward the right ingredients for building a "Gospel Advancing Ministry." What exactly do I mean by a "Gospel Advancing Ministry"? It's a ministry that relentlessly pursues the mission of Jesus by relationally multiplying disciples, resulting in radical gospel transformation.

Let's break down that definition, phrase by phrase, and see if it lines up with the ministry approach God gave us in the book of Acts...

Pursuing the Mission of Jesus

There was a sense of urgency in Acts 1 when the two men dressed in white (angels?), in essence, told the disciples, "Don't just stand there...gospelize!" They were reminding the disciples and all their spiritual descendants—which includes us!—that there is a mission to accomplish, a plan to accomplish it and a deadline to accomplish it by.

Just weeks earlier on a mountain in Galilee, the disciples heard Jesus deliver what many call "The Great Commission" today. I actually prefer to call it "THE Cause," because "The Great Commission" sounds like something a real estate agent came up with. But no matter the label we give it, it's a grand call to an even grander mission!

> *Then the eleven disciples left for Galilee, going to the mountain where Jesus had told them to go. When they saw him, they worshiped him—but some of them doubted!*

> *Jesus came and told his disciples, "I have been given all authority in heaven and on earth. Therefore, go and make disciples of all the nations, baptizing them in the name of the Father and the Son and the Holy Spirit. Teach these new disciples to obey all the commands I have given you. And be sure of this: I am with you always, even to the end of the age"* (Matthew 28:16-20).

I love this passage because it shows that, although the disciples worshipped Jesus, some still had their doubts. Why? Just days earlier they had seen Him mocked, mangled and murdered by Roman soldiers! And now He was before them, telling them He was giving them a job to do!

You may have your doubts too. It's okay. Jesus will use us, doubts and all, if we have faith enough to obey His prime directive to make disciples.

And that's what we're here to do. Are you carrying out the primary mission of making and multiplying disciples through your youth ministry? Are you equipping your teenagers to do the same? Or are you defined more by meetings than by Christ's mission?

Say I tell my son and daughter, Jeremy and Kailey, "I'm going to the store. Before I get back I want you to make your beds." When I leave, I expect them to obey me while I'm gone. If I come back and ask, "Did you make your beds?" and they answer, "Well, no, Dad, but we talked about it with each other quite a bit," or Jeremy says, "I wrote a song about it and taught it to Kailey...can we sing it for you, now?" or "We googled it and found some cool YouTube videos that we studied about the best ways to make a bed," it will not be a happy day in the Stier house. Why? Because despite all the talk, creative talent expended and diligent study, they never actually got around to doing the task that I'd assigned them.

In the same way, Jesus left us with a simple mandate, not to make the bed, but to make disciples. When He returns and asks, "Did you make disciples?" and we answer, "No, but we had a killer youth program," or "Nope, but we sang a song about it," or "Nah, but we googled some great teaching outlines on disciple making and taught them," then we will have failed to accomplish the primary thing that He asked of us.

We see a relentless pursuit of this mission Jesus has given us to reach the lost and make disciples in every chapter of the book of Acts. We see it in...

- **Acts 1:** Jesus commissioned His disciples to be witnesses to the ends of the earth.

- **Acts 2:** Peter preached on the day of Pentecost and 3,000 were added to their number that day.

- **Acts 3:** Peter healed a crippled man and preached the gospel to another crowd.

- **Acts 4:** The entire church prayed, the building shook and they dispersed to share the good news.

- **Acts 5:** *"Nevertheless, more and more men and women believed in the Lord and were added to their number"* (Acts 5:14).

- **Acts 6:** The apostles devoted themselves to preaching and praying exclusively, so that the gospel was not hindered.

- **Acts 7:** Stephen stood up and gave a powerful gospel message and was stoned for it.

- **Acts 8:** Philip chased down a chariot and shared the good news with the Ethiopian Eunuch.

- **Acts 9:** Saul (a.k.a., Paul) got saved and started sharing the gospel with everyone.

- **Acts 10:** A whole group of God-fearing Gentiles, led by Cornelius, came to faith in Christ.

- **Acts 11:** A rogue group of believers started sharing the gospel with full-on non-synagogue-attending Greeks— unheard of up to that point—and many put their faith in Jesus.

- **Acts 12:** *"But the word of God continued to increase and spread"* (Acts 12:24).

- **Acts 13:** Paul and Barnabas were sent off to relentlessly pursue the mission of Jesus on their first missionary journey.

- **Acts 14:** Paul was stoned for preaching the gospel—and kept on preaching afterward!

- **Acts 15:** The preaching of the message of grace was attacked by legalistic Judaizers from within the church, but the gospel would not be held down!

- **Acts 16:** Timothy joined the traveling team of Paul and Silas, and they preached the good news in Philippi, where Paul and Silas were flogged, imprisoned and finally released.

- **Acts 17:** They preached the gospel in Thessalonica, Berea and to the philosophers of Athens.

- **Acts 18:** Paul camped out for a year and a half in Corinth, and saturated the region with the good news.

- **Acts 19:** Paul preached the gospel and trained the believers for two to three years in Ephesus, until a riot forced him to leave town.

- **Acts 20:** Paul recounted his commitment to relentlessly pursuing the mission of Jesus to the elders of Ephesus.

- **Acts 21:** Paul updated James and the elders of Jerusalem about all the Gospel Advancing Ministry that God had done through them on their missionary journeys. He was later arrested.

- **Acts 22:** Paul proclaimed the gospel to the crowd that had him arrested—and they freaked out, of course!

- **Acts 23:** God told Paul that, in spite of his arrest, he would share the gospel in Rome just like he had in Jerusalem.

- **Acts 24:** Paul explained the gospel to Felix, the Roman governor of the region.

- **Acts 25:** Paul stood trial before Festus for preaching the gospel.

- **Acts 26:** King Agrippa ripped Paul for trying to convert him by saying: *"Do you think that in such a short time you can persuade me to be a Christian?"* (Acts 26:28).

- **Acts 27:** Paul was sent to Rome to appear before Caesar for the "crime" of preaching the gospel.

- **Acts 28:** For two years under house arrest, Paul *"proclaimed the kingdom of God and taught about the Lord Jesus Christ—with all boldness and without hindrance!"* (Acts 28:31).

From the first page to the last page of Acts, this book drips with the relentless pursuit of the mission of Jesus. It's a blueprint for what it looks like to gospelize a community, a city, a country and a world.

How do the pages of your youth ministry read? Is your ministry story more about what you're doing, or more about what is getting done when it comes to the gospel changing young lives?

It all starts by choosing to relentlessly pursue the mission of Jesus, but it continues by...

Relationally Multiplying Disciples

"And the word of God continued to increase, and the number of the disciples multiplied greatly in Jerusalem...." (Acts 6:7a, ESV).

Making disciples who make disciples gets talked about a lot in ministry circles, but is not actually done in far too many cases. Yet when it is actually carried out it is truly exciting.

I'll never forget going to The Gathering for the first time. This extraordinary city-wide youth group meeting happens every month in Kenosha, Wisconsin—and this particular month it was being held at Immanuel Baptist Church. This town of 100,000 people is located roughly 45 minutes north of Chicago. Humanly speaking, it might seem like an unlikely place for God to be doing something groundbreaking with His church.

But I'm convinced that He is.

While at The Gathering, I met teenagers who'd been led to Jesus by other teenagers, who'd been led to Jesus by other teenagers. I also met a group of youth leaders who hailed from a variety of churches and denominations, but were united together by their obsessive focus on Jesus and His mission to reach the lost at any cost.

This dynamic youth leader network is known as the Kenosha Allies. These youth leaders—as well as a senior pastor or two thrown in for good measure—meet every week to pray for each other, for the youth in their groups and for their community. Their insatiable thirst for the mission of Jesus will not be quenched until every teenager in their city encounters Jesus Christ personally.

By the way, their meetings are about three hours long. During that time, they eat and pray together. When I visited their network meeting, it was the closest thing I've experienced to a band-of-brothers type gathering.

They hold each other accountable. They support each other's churches. If the smaller churches have a tough time affording an event they are doing together, like a camp, conference or retreat, the bigger churches with bigger budgets will help out financially.

And this is no theologically watered-down, let's-all-just-sing-kumbya-type group. They unite together around the gospel of Jesus Christ. If you have a different gospel than faith alone in Christ alone, they will still love you, but you won't get a ticket to become a leader in this city-wide Gospel Advancing Movement.

But once you become a part of this tight group of multi-flavored Jesus followers, be warned. They will ask you hard questions, pray specifically for the deepest needs of your life and ministry, and then boldly challenge you to get your teenagers reaching their peers for Jesus.

While they all run their own youth ministries in their own churches, they bring all their groups together once a month on a rotating basis at different churches for The Gathering. Right before these large group rallies, they do campus missionary classes for teenagers, including evangelism training. During their main meetings, hundreds of teenagers from the different youth groups represented gather to worship God, pray collectively and be challenged by God's Word to advance Christ's message across Kenosha one teenager at a time.

 #GOSPELIZE *When you make the gospel central to everything you are doing, you are gospelizing your ministry.*

It's the closest thing I've experienced to seeing the book of Acts lived out in a Western youth ministry context.

Led by twin ring leaders, Andy and Roger, the individual youth ministries represented by the Kenosha Allies are vibrant, real life examples of what Gospel Advancing Ministries can look like. But the Kenosha Allies are also a practical demonstration of what a gospel advancing network of youth leaders can look like.

I'll never forget meeting some of the teenagers in Andy's youth group during my visit to The Gathering. While loud Christian music was pulsating across the room, scores of teenagers mingled about laughing and drinking Coke. I took the opportunity to informally interview a handful of teenagers about how they got plugged into the youth ministry. There I discovered that Austin heard the gospel from Alex, who'd been trained to share his faith by Andy. Okay, to be honest, I don't remember the names. But I do remember meeting disciples, who were reached by disciples, who were trained by Andy. He and his crew of student and adult leaders were relationally multiplying disciples.

Andy's youth group was a song-singing, pizza-eating, dodge-ball-dodging example of disciple multiplication. My mind couldn't help but snap back to the book of Acts. It felt just like the early church, but with a better band. It brought to mind Christian rapper, Lecrae's, *After the Music Stops*, where he says, "I'm out to take the Bible, create disciples, who make disciples, disciple-cycles..."[2]

When the Kenosha Allies bestowed on me the title of "Honorary Member," it came as one of the greatest honors of my life, because I believe the model that God has built in Kenosha can multiply in youth groups and networks across the nation and across the world!

The work God is doing in Kenosha can be duplicated in your city and through your youth ministry. The same Holy Spirit that is fueling these youth leaders in Kenosha dwells inside of you and is longing to do a work in your community beyond your wildest dreams!

Resulting in Radical Gospel Transformation

When Jesus confronted and commissioned Saul (Paul) on the road to Damascus, He laid out a brief description of what the powerful message of the gospel would do to and for those who heard it. Jesus said:

> "Now get up and stand on your feet. I have appeared to you to appoint you as a servant and as a witness of what you have seen and will see of me. I will rescue you from your own people and from the Gentiles. I am sending you to them to open their eyes and turn them from darkness to light, and from the power of Satan to God, so that they may receive forgiveness of sins and a place among those who are sanctified by faith in me" (Acts 26:16-18).

Packed in these couple verses are a few quick snapshots of the radical transformation that the gospel brings, not just to the Gentiles Paul would reach, but for the teenagers your student ministry is seeking to reach as well.

The gospel...		
◎	Gives spiritual sight	*"to open their eyes"*
⍟	Brings heavenly light	*"turn them from darkness to light"*
✥	Rescues from Satan's power	*"from the power of Satan to God"*
⌒	Grants God's forgiveness	*"that they may receive forgiveness"*
△	Provides a holy community	*"and a place among those who are sanctified by faith in me."*

What's true of the gospel Paul preached is true of the message we share, because IT'S THE SAME MESSAGE, after all! And THE SAME HOLY SPIRIT who worked through Paul works in us—and our believing teenagers! So there's no reason that this same gospel, working with the same Holy Spirit, shouldn't have the same results!

But Satan whispers in our ears that it's not the same, that Paul's gospel was somehow infused with apostolic superpowers, and that our high-tech, Westernized teenagers are somehow immune to the power of the gospel. He tells us they're too spoiled, too apathetic and too distracted for the gospel to get through to them.

Bologna.

The gospel is as powerful now as it was then, as it ever was, and as it ever will be. And so is the Holy Spirit. He works to convict, convince and convert the unreached to produce radical gospel transformation.

As 2 Thessalonians 2:13-14 reminds us:

> *But we ought always to thank God for you, brothers and sisters loved by the Lord, because God chose you as firstfruits to be saved through the sanctifying work of the Spirit and through belief in the truth. He called you to this through our gospel, that you might share in the glory of our Lord Jesus Christ.*

The power of the Spirit and the power of the gospel work together like nitrogen and glycerin to explosively ignite transformation in the lives of the bad, the broken, the bullied—and the bullies!

It did that for me, for my uncles and even for my mom.

THE WOMAN AT THE WELL (WITH A BASEBALL BAT!)

My mom was married at least four times, though we didn't actually know that until after she died. We found four marriage licenses in her footlocker after her death. As for me, I was the result of a sexual tryst my mom had with a guy named Tony.

I never met Tony. He died long before I even knew that I was the result of little more than a one night stand. Years later, I discovered my biological father was a Sergeant Major in the Army, a POW and the very last prisoner released after the Korean War.

Mom was tightlipped about my father. As a matter of fact, it wasn't until I was 12 years old that I found out anything about Tony at all. Up until then, I just assumed my older brother's dad—who never lived with us, either—was my dad.

But one day, Grandma told me everything.

She told me that after my mom found out she was pregnant with another child that she couldn't afford to raise by herself, she drove from Denver to Boston on the pretense of hanging out with some family members. But her real plan was to have an illegal abortion (this was before Roe vs. Wade), and pretend as if nothing had ever happened.

But the family members she was staying with in Boston got a hold of my grandparents who told my mom, "Come back to Denver, and we'll help you raise that baby."

I was that baby.

For years, I wondered why my mom would frequently burst into tears when she looked at me. I wondered why she would cry almost every night, begging my brother and me not to turn into a "bum" like her. I wondered why she was so full of rage. I once witnessed her taking a baseball bat to the brand new car of her soon-to-be-ex-husband. When he tried to stop her from destroying the car, she turned the baseball bat on him.

So when my grandma told me that my mom almost ended my life in an abortion, I knew immediately that her internal mixture of rage and guilt was a cocktail that would destroy her unless Jesus intervened.

At this point, I was a Christian. And while I was still coming to terms with my father abandoning me/us, I knew I had a heavenly

Father who would never leave me or forsake me. And I knew that the same message that had transformed me could transform her.

So I tried again and again to share the gospel with my mom. But when I told her how Jesus paid the price for her sins on the cross, she would always respond the same way by saying, "You don't know the things I've done wrong."

But I did, because of good old Grandma.

I'd say, "It doesn't matter, Mom. Jesus paid the price for all your sins."

She would always shrug it off, muttering about how God could never forgive her. But one night, while she was smoking her Benson and Hedges Gold cigarettes (filtered, please), I shared the good news one more time. By this time I was fifteen years of age, and had been sharing the message of the gospel with her for years.

She said, "You mean to tell me that Jesus paid for all my sins? Even the really bad ones?"

I said, "Yes, Ma."

She took a drag on her cigarette, thought for a moment and said, "I'm in!"

Mom put her faith in Jesus right there and then. She had her eyes opened, and she went *"from darkness to light, and from the power of Satan to God."* She received God's forgiveness and a place among God's people. My mom experienced radical gospel transformation.

And so did I…because God used me—a fifteen-year-old, dirt poor teenager—to rescue my mom from a life of guilt and sin. From that point forward, I watched the gospel message transform her from the inside out. I witnessed her boldness in sharing her faith with her coworkers, our neighbors and complete strangers. She wanted to make sure that she shared this same good news with everyone she could.

It's been over a decade ago since I sat by her bed in hospice and watched my mom die. Even then, with her body decimated by stage four lung cancer, her soul was alive with hope. Nurse after nurse heard the good news, because my mom would whisper to them, "My son has something to tell you," which was code for me to share the gospel with them.

Radical gospel transformation is something very personal to me. The message transformed me from a scared, scarred, fatherless kid from the city, into a bold witness who knew God was his Daddy. It transformed my mom from a guilt-ridden, fist-clenching rage-aholic, into the most authentic, generous and blunt witness for Jesus you could ever imagine. I watched my once violent family metamorphosed into a family that became a shining light of hope to a community steeped in crime and brokenness.

And it all started because a Gospel Advancing Ministry in Arvada, Colorado, reached out to the inner city to bring the good news to my family and me. They were relentless in their pursuit of the mission of Jesus, and we were reached as a result. They relationally multiplied disciples, and I was one of them...and I got to reach my mom, and she reached countless others! The result? Radical gospel transformation in our lives, family and community!

What we read in the dusty pages of Acts needs to be dusted off and done again today in our 21st century postmodern context. Why? Because the mission is clear, and the deadline is near. Like it says in Acts 1:11, He will be coming back!

So don't just stand there...gospelize!

SPICE IT UP...

Questions to help you and your leaders "Gospelize YOUR Youth Ministry."

1. Do you think we are currently more of a "standing around looking up at the sky" type of youth group, or a "step out and gospelize" type of youth group?

2. On a scale of one to ten, where do you think our youth ministry currently falls in terms of our effectiveness in advancing the gospel? Why do you think that?

3. Discuss Greg's definition of a Gospel Advancing Ministry as one that "relentlessly pursues the mission of Jesus by relationally multiplying disciples, resulting in radical gospel transformation." Is there anything about this definition that you would change?

4. Let's talk about each phrase of this definition. On a scale of one to ten, how do you think our youth ministry is currently doing at "pursuing the mission of Jesus"? Why do you think that?

5. What impact did Greg's rundown of the relentless pursuit of the lost in every chapter of the book of Acts have on you personally? Did it make you feel motivated, guilty, bored, knowledgeable or something else?

6. On a scale of one to ten, where do you think we currently fall in terms of making and multiplying disciples?

7. Is our ministry currently more effective at advancing the gospel **in** our students, or **through** our students? Discuss the difference between the two.

8. What did you think of Greg's contention that "there's no reason that this same gospel, working with the same Holy Spirit, shouldn't have the same results!"?

9. Have you ever personally led someone to faith in Jesus? Did it have the kind of effect of transforming **both** them and you that Greg talked about experiencing with his mom?

10. At this point, do the concepts being presented in this book seem intriguing or overwhelming or both?

CHAPTER 02

THE ~~LAST~~ LOST CHAPTER OF ACTS

Have you ever read the book of Acts, and then gone to church right afterward? Let's be honest, if you attend a typical church, the comparison between the two generally translates into a huge disappointment.

Why? Because as you read the book of Acts, you can actually feel the pulsating heart of the early church! There is an overwhelming sense of mission, excitement, risk and even danger. And over all of these new believers, there was a warm blanket of inescapable love—love for God and love for others.

This love demonstrated itself in a generosity that was so deep and rich that the 1st century believers selflessly shared their possessions. You see this powerfully demonstrated in Acts 2. Many of these newly converted Jewish believers in Jesus had traveled from great distances to Jerusalem to celebrate the Feast of Pentecost, also known as the Festival of Shavu'ot or the Feast of Weeks. This was the second of three major festivals that every able-bodied Jewish male was required to attend (Exodus 23:16).

Think about the planning required to attend this feast. You would bring enough food and money for the trip, though probably not much more than the bare minimum. But if you were one of the 3,000 Jewish men who put their faith in Jesus when Peter preached on the day of Pentecost as recorded in Acts 2:41, you very likely wouldn't want to leave the party. Because of your newfound faith, you'd want to stay extra weeks, maybe even months, to learn more about Jesus.

So the selflessness of the early believers kicked into full gear. They dug deep into their own pockets to give you extra money for food, lodging and expenses. These self-sacrificing Jewish believers made it possible for you to stay longer and grow deeper in your faith, before you shuttled back to your own hometown, taking the good news with you! And when you returned home, you'd be fully equipped to spread the gospel in your own community!

Maybe that's one reason why there was already a firmly established church in Italy when Paul arrived there under Roman guard on his final trip to Rome in Acts 28:14-15. What is highly intriguing about the final chapter of Acts is that it leaves you dangling, like a cliffhanger. Acts 28:30-31 simply says:

> *For two whole years Paul stayed there in his own rented house and welcomed all who came to see him. He proclaimed the kingdom of God and taught about the Lord Jesus Christ—with all boldness and without hindrance!*

Okay.

That's it?

What about Paul's execution? What about the church's spread beyond Italy? What about the great persecution under Nero?

Nada.

It just leaves us hanging there.

Personally, I think there's a divine reason for this incomplete story. The Holy Spirit is writing a script through the pen of Luke that is meant to feel unfinished because, in a sense, it is. We are the continuation of the book of Acts!

Look at what the good Dr. Luke wrote at the very beginning of this amazing book:

> *In my first book I told you, Theophilus, about everything Jesus* ***began to do and teach*** *until the day he was taken up to heaven after giving his chosen apostles further instructions through the Holy Spirit* (Acts 1:1-2).

As the classic expositor Alexander MacLaren wrote:

> Is not the natural inference that the latter treatise will tell us what Jesus *continued* 'to do and teach' *after* He was taken up? I think so. And thus the writer sets forth at once, for those that have eyes to see, what he means to do, and what he thinks his book is going to be about.[1]

Though Luke put his pen down at the end of Acts 28, the Holy Spirit is still writing a story in and through us! Although it's not part of the canon of Scripture, and cannot be found on any human parchment, it is the story of church history that continues on today!

And you and your youth group are part of it!

After all, the book of Acts is really not just the Acts of the early church. It's actually the Acts of Jesus through His Holy Spirit working through the church! And He is still working today! His plan is to advance His kingdom deeply into the hearts of your teenagers, and deeply into the heart of your community.

Colossians 1:6 puts it like this:

> ...*In the same way, the gospel is bearing fruit and growing throughout the whole world—just as it has been doing among you since the day you heard it and truly understood God's grace.*

And just like it did in the church of Colossae, the gospel will produce fruit in your teenagers and through your teenagers, as they take the good news message to their peers.

So, if the book of Acts, in a sense, is still being written, how do you get that same dynamic, enthusiastic spirit of gospel advancement infused into your youth group? Well, in a very theological way, that same Holy Spirit is infused in the hearts of all of your believing teenagers! And that same gospel that the early disciples proclaimed, your teenagers are called to share! And when your teenagers begin to spread this good news, something very surprising begins to happen; they begin to grow in their faith in ways you never expected.

BOMB DEFUSING CLASS

Imagine that I talked with your church leadership, and they agreed that if you wanted to keep your job you had to sit through a six week, 12-hour-a-day bomb defusing class led by a team of bomb disposal experts. You didn't have to pass the class to keep your job, but you did have to sit through it. Most likely, after the awe of realizing you were in a bomb defusing class wore off, you'd start to realize how many math, chemistry and engineering principles you were going to have to listen to. At that point, you'd probably begin to lose interest. Soon, you'd be checking your Twitter feed, texting friends, playing games on your phone or doodling—anything but tuning into this boring class on bombs!

Now, let's say we change the scenario a bit. Let's say that at the beginning of the class I told you that after six weeks of training you were going to go over to the Middle East and defuse bombs for the United States Army. How well do you think you would listen then? Of course, you'd pay close attention, take copious notes and stay after class to ask questions of the bomb defusing experts. "Was it the red wire or green wire we cut in that scenario?" Why? Because you knew you would soon be in the hurt locker and could die if you weren't trained and ready!

Without the prospect of getting plunged into the danger, the six week class would have been just a boring exercise in chemistry, mathematics and wire cutting. But with the prospect of actually needing this knowledge to accomplish your life or death mission, everything changes.

In the same way, many of your teenagers feel like they're stuck in a six week long, boring Bible class when they go to youth group. For many of them, it can sound like an exercise in dusty theology and ancient Bible studies. But if they know that you are going to lovingly, but relentlessly, challenge them to share the gospel with their peers—the Christian version of bomb defusing—there's a good chance they are going to study the Bible extra hard and pray even harder! And all of this will help them grow deeper in their relationship with God.

MY BIG AHA!

I've talked to thousands of youth leaders about mobilizing their teenagers to share the gospel. I often get a response that goes something like this: "Of course, I'd love for my teenagers to share Jesus with their peers, but they're not quite ready yet."

I usually respond by asking, "So you're saying they need more theology, more small group lessons and more Sunday school teaching?"

"Yeah, they need more spiritual growth before they're ready to share their faith," these youth leaders confirm, as they nod in agreement.

Then I ask this simple question: "How's that worked out for the adults in your church?"

There's typically a dramatic pause before they offer up a sheepish nod, as the lights go on and they get my point.

If teaching, training, theology, Sunday school, small groups and ministry meetings resulted in a lifestyle of evangelism, our churches would be filled with evangelizing adults. But, sadly, they're not.

I believe it's significant that the first act of a new believer in the early church was water baptism. You see this in Acts 2, when 3,000 put their faith in Jesus and were baptized as a result of hearing Peter's Pentecost sermon. In their day, the act of water baptism was no private ritual. Because there were no church buildings in the 1st century, baptisms happened in very public places like rivers, lakes or maybe even the southern steps of the temple where ceremonial Jewish baths are carved into the rock to this day. In other words, your unbelieving family, friends, coworkers and countrymen would most likely be witnesses to your public declaration of your newfound faith—and this was in an era where many considered Christianity some kind of cult.

In light of this reality, Romans 10:9 takes on newfound significance when it says: *"If you declare with your mouth, 'Jesus is Lord,' and believe in your heart that God raised him from the dead, you will be saved."*

Here's how the text notes of *The NIV Study Bible* (1985 edition) puts it:

> **Jesus is Lord.** The earliest Christian confession of faith (cf. 1 Co 12:30), probably used at baptisms. In view of the fact that "Lord" (Greek *kyrios*) is used over 6,000 times in the Septuagint (the Greek translation of the OT) to translate the name of Israel's god (Yahweh), it is clear that Paul, when using this word of Jesus is ascribing deity to him.[2]

To recognize the Lordship of Jesus was to recognize Him as God in the flesh. To verbally proclaim, "Jesus is Lord" was considered blasphemous by the Jews and treasonous by the Romans. Because Jews were monotheistic—meaning they believed in only one God—and because they had no concept of the Trinity, many Jews viewed this simple three word description of Jesus as heresy to the highest degree.

Because Romans viewed the Emperor as Lord—as deity—they sometimes tried to force early Christians to say, "Caesar is Lord." If these Christians refused, they would either be mutilated or murdered. This was the case with Polycarp, a disciple of St. John. Under intense pressure, he refused to say, "Caesar is Lord," because he believed only Jesus was Lord. At the age of 86, he was burned at the stake because of his convictions.

In the early church, the phrase, "Jesus is Lord," was powerfully catalytic in the culture, and potentially catastrophic for the Christian. If you lived at this time and proclaimed, "Jesus is Lord," at a minimum you could be put out of your social circle, and at the maximum, you could be put out of existence.

The very act of being baptized was a declaration that "Jesus is Lord." Imagine the gospel advancing impact it had! When new believers were baptized, their verbal affirmation of the deity of Jesus became a huge evangelistic opportunity. I wonder how many believers we will meet in heaven who converted to Christianity as a result of witnessing someone else's baptism, triggered by the proclamation, "Jesus is Lord"?

Imagine the spiritual courage it would take for a new believer to make such a bold statement in front of potentially antagonistic strangers and friends, while standing in the water about to get baptized. This proclamation could get them killed. But it also steeled and sealed their newfound faith in a very powerful way.

My big aha is that when teenagers declare to their pluralistic, "mix-and-match," postmodern peers that "Jesus is Lord," it will do more to accelerate their spiritual growth than ten years worth of Bible lessons. It causes them to put skin in the game, because they risk losing their social status. And it is this very risk that is the core to the call of discipleship.

I am convinced from the whole of the New Testament AND from personal experience, that injecting a gospel advancing philosophy into a youth group will accelerate the discipleship process faster than just about anything else. Why? Because it shifts the perspective from "my needs" to "God's call." Plus, on a personal level, it challenges teenagers to risk their relationships for something of eternal significance, it drives them toward reliance on the Spirit and it pushes them to obey God.

RISKING RELATIONSHIPS

Yet at the same time many even among the leaders believed in him. But because of the Pharisees they would not openly acknowledge their faith for fear they would be put out of the synagogue; for they loved human praise more than praise from God (John 12:42-43).

Here's an example of some early believers who had put their faith in Jesus, but refused to publicly acknowledge it. Why? Because they didn't want to risk their relationships with other leaders and their status in the community!

While some may say these were not true believers, I would remind you that the Holy Spirit's commentary on their hearts is that they had believed, but weren't willing to go that next step. In the same way, many believing teenagers in your youth group have never taken the next step of sharing their faith with their peers because *"they loved the praise of man more than the praise of God."*

But central to the call of discipleship is the call to relational risk. Jesus told His own disciples in Matthew 10:37-39:

> *"Anyone who loves their father or mother more than me is not worthy of me; anyone who loves their son or daughter more than me is not worthy of me. Whoever does not take up their cross and follow me is not worthy of me. Whoever finds their life will lose it, and whoever loses their life for my sake will find it."*

What's striking about this passage is that it specifically comes in the context of Jesus unleashing His followers on an evangelistic campaign (Matthew 10:1-7). As He sends the twelve out, Jesus is reminding them that following Him involves sacrifice, including risking even their closest, most important relationships. He's calling them to take up their cross, and willingly die a social death—and perhaps even a physical one—for His sake!

In some situations, sharing Jesus' message may offend father, mother, sister, brother and friend. It may even fracture relationships. But the very act of embracing this kind of social risk will yield an incalculable reward—true, abundant life with deep significance—a life of growing, maturing and thriving in Christ!

THE "MY STORY" MOVEMENT

I lead a ministry called Dare 2 Share (D2S) that provides gospel advancing training for youth leaders and teens all across the country.

After I speak at a D2S teen training conference, I get hungry. And this particular night, I was famished. As you know, speaking to teenagers is an exhausting and exhilarating undertaking. Unlike adults, they won't just nod their heads and pretend like they are enjoying your talk. They will get up and leave, or just start texting and talking with those around them if they find you boring.

This can be nerve-wracking on communicators like me who speak to tens of thousands of teenagers every year. Usually I don't eat much before I speak, but I go out and eat way too much after. The nervousness and pressure that comes with preaching to teenagers generally makes my stomach nauseous beforehand and famished afterward.

One particular night in Eden Prairie, Minnesota, I was headed to a local Ruby Tuesday. I had invited my good friend, Dave, to go out with me. He was the missions pastor at a local church and embodied a gospel advancing lifestyle more consistently than anybody I had ever met.

While we were there getting ready to order, his daughter called and asked if she and a few friends could come by. They had been at the Dare 2 Share conference too.

Soon, about eight teenagers crashed our party. All of these students, most of whom were star athletes at Eden Prairie High School, were fired up about reaching their school for Jesus. Dave had been coaching them in relational evangelism, and they were praying for their friends and sharing their faith. Gospel conversations were happening everywhere. And now they were working on a plan to pray for every student on campus by name, initiate even more spiritual conversations and close out the school year with a major outreach event. This event would be called "My Story," because a few of the Christian student leaders would be sharing their faith at the event in a very public and powerful way.

Dave had helped line up some special guests—a few Minnesota Vikings football players and a former gangsta rapper who was now rapping for Jesus. But the real stars of the "My Story" program would be the teenagers. These high school athletes were putting their reputations on the line, not only when they stood to share their story in front of their peers, but in the many gospel conversations they'd have leading up to the event and after it!

Today the "My Story" movement is gaining momentum as more and more teenagers at more and more schools are standing in front of their peers to share their story of salvation. This year they not only packed out the Eden Prairie High School auditorium (where 106 students indicated a decision to put their trust in Jesus!), but they did four other events in the Twin Cities area where many more became believers in Jesus!

It's their prayer that the movement will spread to campuses across the country. And the exciting thing is that it's not about any one church or organization. It is a kingdom initiative which is all about Jesus. Students are sharing their faith story with their peers so they can engage in spiritual conversations and share the gospel.

But in addition to the many who have been transformed by the gospel of Jesus through these events, something else more subtle, but just as powerful, has been taking place. The faith of the teenagers driving these conversations is growing deeper and richer. They are seeing the lives of their friends transformed. They are, in some cases, experiencing a mild form of persecution which deepens their faith even more. They are witnessing firsthand the power of the Spirit. For these students, Christianity has moved from theoretical Sunday school lessons, to hardcore, life-giving reality.

CULTIVATING RELIANCE ON GOD

I'll never forget when Tim Keller tweeted this: "Teenagers have more information about God than they have experiences of him. Get them in places where they have to rely on God."[3]

Maybe that's why Jesus sent His disciples out on their first solo evangelistic campaign without anything else to rely on but the Holy Spirit. In Matthew 10:9-10, Jesus said: *"Do not get any gold or silver or copper to take with you in your belts—no bag for the journey or extra shirt or sandals or a staff, for the worker is worth his keep."*

So they had no extra money to bank on, no extra clothes to put on and no walking stick to lean on or use as a defense if they were attacked by wild animals along the way! They only had the Holy Spirit. And a little later in this same passage, Jesus again instructed them to rely fully on the Spirit by telling them: *"At that time you will be given what to say, for it will not be you speaking, but the Spirit of your Father speaking through you"* (Matthew 10:19-20).

In the same way, when you put your teenagers in a position of having to trust God, their theological information about God is activated, as their spiritual dependence on Him is accelerated. If you've ever taken your teenagers on a mission trip to a foreign country, especially in the developing world, you've probably seen this clearly demonstrated.

But, in a very real sense, your teenagers go on a mission trip every day when they walk into their schools. And, for many of them, this is a scarier trip than traveling hundreds or thousands of miles to some dangerous, foreign country.

If you give teenagers a choice between going on a mission trip to the Amazon where they might have to fight off jaguars and pythons while building a mud hut for an obscure Indian tribe, or going into their school cafeteria to sit with a group of their peers and try to bring the gospel up, I'm convinced most would choose the Amazon. Why? Because the majority of teenagers I've met would rather risk getting choked by a python, than risk getting choked out of their social circle! The very thought of sharing Jesus with their classmates, teammates and friends triggers a palpating heart and knocking knees.

But knocking knees are more likely to bend to God in prayerful reliance.

I've seen this demonstrated again and again at the Dare 2 Share conferences across America. After we train teenagers to share the good news, we have them hold their cell phones up high into the air. And then we have them call or text their friends and initiate a gospel conversation. Many of them give me that "Are you serious?" look as it begins to sink in that I'm actually asking them to do this totally out of their comfort zone thing. That look quickly turns into a "Holy crap, you are serious!" look.

But before I have them call or text their friends, we pray. And you can feel the prayers going up, because for many of these teenagers, this is the first time they've been put in a position of risk. As a result, many of these teenagers are praying like they haven't prayed in a long time.

When's the last time you, like Jesus, put His followers in your youth group in a position to risk? Like Tim Keller said, they have plenty of information about God. It's time we put them in a position where they have to trust in Him. Relational evangelism does just that!

 #GOSPELIZE *Knocking knees are more likely to bend to God in prayerful reliance.*

THE CALL TO OBEY

In the 21st century version of Westernized Christianity, discipleship is a flash drive. We insert said truth into the minds of our teenagers, download it and move on. It's almost as though we think that Jesus' directive to His disciples in Matthew 28:19 was, "teaching them everything I commanded you...," instead of *"teaching them **to obey** everything I commanded you...."*

We tend to have a knowledge-based, instead of a heart-based and action-based version of discipling teenagers—and adults for that matter! As a result, we think that all we must do is teach them more and more. If they get more theology and Bible and Christian worldview, then everything will be fine.

While all these truths are vitally important, they must not *just* be understood on a head level. They must be rigorously applied to their hearts and lives. They must be embraced and obeyed.

And when our teenagers embrace God's call and obey Him, especially in the face of personal loss, the discipleship process is accelerated in a way no Bible study can replicate.

Consider the example of Abraham's obedience and sacrifice in Old Testament times:

> *Was not our father Abraham considered righteous for what he did when he offered his son Isaac on the altar? You see that his faith and his actions were working together, and his faith was made complete by what he did* (James 2:21-22).

What's interesting about this passage is that James is writing about an incident that took place twenty plus years after *"Abraham believed and it was counted to him as righteousness"* (Genesis 15:6).

Decades after Abraham was justified (declared righteous) spiritually, he was declared righteous in a different way. Because he was willing to obey God by sacrificing what meant most to him on the altar—his son Isaac—he was declared righteous *practically.*

The first declaration of righteousness in Genesis 15 meant he was saved. The second declaration of righteousness in Genesis 22 meant he had spiritually matured to the point where the "angel of the Lord"—most likely the pre-incarnate Christ—said: *"Do not do anything to him. Now I know that you fear God, because you have not withheld from me your son, your only son"* (Genesis 22:12).

The first declaration of righteousness was because Abraham believed the promise of God in Genesis 15:16. The second declaration of righteousness was because Abraham believed and backed it up with obedience, by demonstrating his willingness to sacrifice what meant most to him on the altar.

As a result, Abraham's own spiritual maturity was accelerated. *"His faith and his actions were working together and his faith was made complete* ("matured") *by what he did."*

So how does this crash course in the Old Testament story of Abraham help make a case for the infusion of a gospel advancing focus being a powerful discipleship accelerator? If Abraham's faith was matured by his willingness to sacrifice what meant most to him on the altar, then the same is true of your teenagers! When they, like Abraham, obey God by being willing to risk a friendship if need be, because they are passionate about sharing the gospel with their peers, their faith and their actions work together, so that their faith is matured in a deep and lasting way.

The reality of a potential loss of friendship or social status looms over a teenager about to share their faith like loss loomed over Abraham on Mt. Moriah that day so long ago. But it is the very possibility of loss that can result in young people taking an Abrahamic step of faith and obedience. This is when their faith becomes more than just lip service. It becomes faith that will sanctify them more quickly. That's why a gospel advancing focus—especially when they're sharing the gospel with their friends, family, classmates and teammates—accelerates the spiritual maturity process in your teenagers faster than just about anything.

BRING ACTS BACK!

You and your believing teenagers have the same Holy Spirit that the apostles did. In fact, you could make the case that you even have more than they did, because you have the complete canon of Scripture and 2,000 years of church history to learn from—both good and bad.

What if you decided that through God's power you were going to prayerfully lead the way for Acts-like, gospel advancing transformation in your church and community? What if you decided that you're tired of reading about revivals of the past, and wanted to be a part of one here and now? What if you led the way for carrying on what the early disciples started, and you pushed to complete the task before Jesus returns?

Now is the time, and you are the leader! Your teenagers are waiting for someone to lead them toward a life of significance, and you are the person God has strategically placed in their lives to challenge, encourage and equip them to get there!

When you choose to do this and decide, by God's grace, to lead your teenagers to be Jesus-focused, gospel advancing, disciple-multiplying believers, they will spiritually grow beyond your wildest imagination!

Don't wait for "when they're ready," because they will grow as they go…and so will you! And the final result will be a walking, talking, living, breathing, Spirit-infused atmosphere of Acts in your youth group, in your teenagers and in your community! And years from now, if someone chronicles the transformation of your city, they may write of your youth group: *"And each day the Lord added to their fellowship those who were being saved"* (Acts 2:47).

SPICE IT UP...

Questions to help you and your leaders "Gospelize *YOUR* Youth Ministry."

1. Do you agree with Greg that the church today has lost much of the passion for the gospel that the early church displayed in the book of Acts? Why or why not?

2. Is our youth ministry currently driven by a sense of mission, excitement and risk? Why do think that?

3. Is there a "warm blanket of inescapable love—love for God and love for others" encircling our youth ministry?

4. What did you think of the bomb defusing class illustration?

5. Do you agree or disagree that taking relational risks for the sake of Jesus triggers spiritual growth?

6. When's the last time you personally put yourself in a position of social risk for Jesus' sake?

7. When's the last time we, like Jesus, challenged the students in our youth group to take a social risk for Jesus' sake?

8. Discuss Tim Keller's quote: "Teenagers have more information about God than they have experiences of him. Get them in places where they have to rely on God."

9. What are the implications for our youth group of Greg's statement: "It's almost as though we think that Jesus' directive to His disciples in Matthew 28:19 was, "teaching them everything I commanded you...," instead of *"teaching them **to** obey everything I commanded you...."*

10. How does relational evangelism give teenagers a taste of "Abrahamic-type faith"?

CHAPTER 03

MEXICAN FOOD AND YOUTH MINISTRY

"What is a burrito?" "Tortilla with cheese, meat, and vegetables." "Well, then, what is a tostada?" "Tortilla with cheese, meat, and vegetables." "Well, then, what i-" "Look, it's all the same XS@*!... Mexican food is great, but it is all the same, it's almost a conspiracy. It's almost like they had a meeting 200 years ago in Mexico City, and one guy stood up, and he was like, "Hey, the reason I got everyone here is pretty simple, I figured we could rename this one entree seven times, and sell it to the North Americans."

—Jim Gaffigan[1]

The full-length version of this standup comedy routine by Jim Gaffigan is absolutely hilarious! But I suspect that ever since you first looked at the cover of this book, you've been wondering what a chili pepper has to do with gospelizing your youth ministry.

Well, in the same way that a lot of Mexican food is made from the same basic ingredients, every Gospel Advancing Ministry has seven basic ingredients that can be mixed together in a variety of different ways. From these ingredients, some will make a "taco" type youth ministry. Others will serve up a "burrito" type ministry. Still others may create something more along the lines of a "tostada." But they all incorporate seven ingredients—or values, if you will—as part of the recipe in some way and to one degree or another with the gospel itself infusing the spiciness. As you mix these ingredients together in your own unique way with the gospel as the "kick," they create a dynamic, spicy dish that gets people so excited that they want to share it with others.

That's one of the things that I love about building a gospelized youth ministry. You can do it in your own context, and creatively reflect your own tastes. Because the gospel itself provides the "kick," there's not a strict, prescriptive recipe that forces you to cook your dish one specific way in order to mass produce a uniform end product. You can freely experiment, borrow from other's recipes, and creatively blend these seven basic ingredients together. Once you make a dish that works for your particular youth ministry setting, you can share that recipe with others, so they can try your approach or customize

SHARE YOUR IDEAS! *To share your own gospel advancing ideas with other youth leaders go to gospeladvancing.com.*

it as they see fit, as well. Your recipe will reflect your own strategies, programs and resources that will best incorporate these seven ingredients/values in your particular setting.

So you know, I didn't develop these values. I discovered them. They've shown themselves, again and again, to be true statistically, scripturally and strategically. Let me explain.

Statistically: A few years ago, Dare 2 Share commissioned a national research project that evaluated the effectiveness of youth ministries evangelistically. About 10% of those surveyed had a new conversion growth rate of 25% or more per year. In other words, a full quarter of their annual growth was due to non-Christian teenagers putting their faith in Jesus and getting plugged into the youth group. As we analyzed the research, it became more and more clear that the highest performing youth ministries embodied these seven values.

Scripturally: After identifying these seven values in our survey results, I crosschecked them scripturally, specifically with the Gospels and the book of Acts. I was greatly encouraged by the number of passages that affirmed these same seven values. I'll be unpacking many of these passages in the coming chapters of this book.

Strategically: I've spent over 25 years in ministry as a youth leader, church planter and youth ministry para-church leader. Across those years and roles, I've labored to strategically inject a gospel advancing philosophy into each. In my role as founder and CEO of Dare 2 Share, I've engaged with thousands of youth leaders across the nation. And here's my practical, frontlines observation: I have tasted these seven ingredients in every ministry dish worth biting into.

Should I have been surprised? No, actually. Why? Because Jesus embedded all of these values into His earthly ministry. And He passed them on to the early disciples. Over the intervening 2,000 years, they've been adopted and adapted in countless variations across cultures and eras—in multitudes of different recipes that incorporate the same basic ingredients.

Sometimes it's easy to forget that Jesus was—and is—just as active after He took His place at the right hand of God, as He was when He was seated next to ordinary men. (Actually He's more active now, because He doesn't have to sleep anymore!) So the book of Acts is our glimpse into how His followers, in the power of His Spirit, blended these seven values together to fit their times and radically changed the world.

The explosive growth of the early church gives clues and cues that can help you experience that same brand of spiritual and numeric growth in your ministries. If you want to learn how to grow your ministry, the book of Acts gives you a crash course!

In the chapters ahead, I'll be diving deeper into each of these seven values. But before I drill down into each one individually, I want to give you a brief overview of the seven and a quick explanation for why I believe these values drove the advancement of the gospel in the book of Acts.

VALUE #1: INTERCESSORY PRAYER FUELS IT.

"They all joined together constantly in prayer...." (Acts 1:14).

Prayer is the first thing the disciples did after Jesus ascended. They met with Him in the heavenlies through relentless prayer. This snapshot of their commitment to pray constantly should demonstrate to us that we too need to join together and pray fervently and consistently.

Yes, they were waiting for the promised Holy Spirit, but shouldn't we wait on the Lord to fill us with His wisdom and fuel us with

His power, as well? Yes, we already have all the Holy Spirit we are ever going to get (Ephesians 1:13-14), but perhaps the more important question is: does He have all of us (Ephesians 5:18)?

We must pray. We must pray for each other and for the lost. We must pray for our churches and our communities. We must pray until our knees are numb and our voices are hoarse. We must pray until God answers.

This intentional and intensive brand of prayer will keep us dependent on Him, strengthen our faith muscles and produce results that can only be explained by divine intervention.

Isn't this what the disciples saw modeled in Jesus' life and ministry again and again and again?

And the early church carried this same passion for prayer. Acts 2:42 says that *"they devoted themselves to the apostles' teaching and to fellowship, to the breaking of bread and to prayer."* Prayer was a key part of their meetings. It wasn't served as an appetizer or a dessert, but was part of the main course.

When we pray and teach our students to pray, we are connecting them with the One who can transform not only their lives, but the lives of their friends, classmates, teammates, family members and coworkers. When prayer becomes the engine, and not the caboose of our youth ministry efforts, then we'll start getting serious traction toward building Gospel Advancing Ministries.

How much does this brand of divine dialogue dominate your life and the lives of your teenagers? Do you have a rhythm of prayer that is relentlessly consistent, or do you use prayer as a kind of holy water, to sprinkle on situations that feel like they're beyond your human capacity to manage and need God's touch?

VALUE #2: RELATIONAL EVANGELISM DRIVES IT.

"…When Priscilla and Aquila heard him [Apollos], *they invited him to their home and explained to him the way of God more adequately"* (Acts 18:26b).

I love the way the Bible gives you insights into issues without being overt. This short, subtle verse gives us a snapshot into how relational evangelism was done in the early church by the "non-rock stars"—those who didn't have the kind of public persona of the more widely known apostles like Paul, Peter and Philip.

What Priscilla and Aquila did in this passage is a picture of relational evangelism at its finest—or maybe discipleship, depending on your view of whether Apollos may have possibly already been a "theologically confused" believer at this point.

First of all, they listened to him. They took time out of their busy lives to try to understand who he was and what he believed.

Secondly, they identified the gaps in his understanding. Whether or not Apollos was saved at this point is up for debate among some Bible scholars, but what's not up for debate is that he was missing some key elements of the good news in his theology.

Thirdly, *"they invited him into their home and explained to him the way of God more adequately."* It was a big deal in this culture to invite someone over to your house. It was a sign of acceptance, hospitality and love. They didn't jump on him and beat him with their gospel bats. They lovingly helped him see the gaps in what he believed, and Apollos consequently became a powerful ambassador of the gospel in the hands of God. Acts 18:27-28 gives us a glimpse of the impact Apollos went on to have:

> When Apollos wanted to go to Achaia, the brothers and sisters encouraged him and wrote to the disciples there to welcome him. When he arrived, he was a great help to those who by grace

had believed. For he vigorously refuted his Jewish opponents in public debate, proving from the Scriptures that Jesus was the Messiah.

In the same way, you must help your teenagers learn how to pull "an Aquila and Priscilla" with their friends. They need to know how to listen, find the critical gaps in other's understanding of the good news, and then explain *"the way of God"* to them more accurately.

As you coach your teenagers to engage their peers with the right mixture of love and boldness, they will see more and more of their friends, classmates and teammates transformed by the gospel.

VALUE #3: LEADERS FULLY EMBRACE AND MODEL IT.

The Spirit of God enabled the leaders of the early church in Acts to live the life and preach the truth that Jesus had modeled for them over the previous three and a half years.

Jesus made it clear in Luke 6:40: *"The student is not above the teacher, but everyone who is fully trained will be like their teacher."* The disciples were bold in proclaiming the truth, because *Jesus* modeled boldness in proclaiming the truth.

The same is true of you with your teenagers. If you're teenagers are not engaged in prayer and relational evangelism, you need a mirror, not a bullhorn, because it starts with you, not them.

 #GOSPELIZE *If you're teenagers are not engaged in prayer and relational evangelism, you need a mirror, not a bullhorn.*

As someone once said, "No tears in the eyes of the writer, no tears in the eyes of the reader."[2] What's true of writing is true of evangelism in the context of a youth group. If the youth leader— and the adult and student leaders—don't have hearts that are broken for the lost, then neither will the teenagers in the youth group. And if those in leadership aren't personally engaging in gospel conversations with others, then the students very likely won't be either.

We must model prayer, spiritual growth, evangelism and disciple multiplication to our teenagers if we expect them to grow in these areas. We don't have to be perfect at it, but we must be making forward progress toward the goal. As we do, our teenagers will follow our lead and become more and more like us, as we become more and more like Jesus.

Soon we will be able to say to them like the Apostle Paul said to the Corinthian believers: *"Follow my example, as I follow the example of Christ"* (1 Corinthians 11:1).

VALUE #4: A DISCIPLE MULTIPLICATION STRATEGY GUIDES IT.

In the book of Acts, there were two types of spiritual movements, one obvious and the other under the surface. The obvious movement was seen when the apostles led hundreds, or even thousands, to Christ through their public preaching, as they did in Acts 2 and 3.

But the other movement, although less obvious, had even more impact in advancing the gospel. This second movement was demonstrated during Paul's time with the Thessalonians, and later with the Ephesians in Acts 19:8-10. The power of the second movement was exponential. It centered on people reaching their own peers with the good news and multiplying the reach of the message as the result of more and more disciples sharing the gospel in their relational circles of influence, until entire regions were saturated with the good news. The results are described by Paul in 1 Thessalonians 1:6-8:

> *You became imitators of us and of the Lord, for you welcomed the message in the midst of severe suffering with the joy given by the Holy Spirit. And so you became a model to all the believers in Macedonia and Achaia. The Lord's message rang out from you not only in Macedonia and Achaia—your faith in God has become known everywhere. Therefore we do not need to say anything about it.*

This regional saturation with the good news was not the result of any super apostle, but of everyday people sharing the good news relationally! The Thessalonians demonstrated this at its finest. They were mimicking Jesus (1 Thessalonians 1:6), modeling joyful endurance to other believers (1 Thessalonians 1:7) and multiplying disciples to share the good news with everyone in their spheres of influence.

Are you leading this "second movement" with your teenagers? Too many times, believers lean on evangelistic "professionals" like the youth leader, guest speaker, evangelist, pastor and so on, to do all of the evangelism. But the real opportunity for advancing the gospel among this generation lies in getting your teenagers to share the good news with their peers.

As your teenagers engage friends, classmates, teammates, coworkers and family members, the Word of the Lord will ring out across your community. This approach to relationally multiplying disciples may not be as sexy as a big outreach, complete with bands, speakers and flashing lights. But in the long run, it has the potential for a much broader reach.

VALUE #5: A BOLD VISION FOCUSES IT.

"But you will receive power when the Holy Spirit comes on you; and you will be my witnesses in Jerusalem, and in all Judea and Samaria, and to the ends of the earth" (Acts 1:8).

I'm convinced that the boldest vision of all time started with Jesus Himself. His goal was that the gospel would be taken *"to the ends of the earth,"* and that disciples would be made and multiplied in every tribe and nation (Matthew 28:19).

Do you have a bold vision for your local community, for every part of your city and for the ends of the earth? Is that bold vision driving your youth ministry efforts across the street (your "Jerusalem" and "Judea"), across the tracks (your "Samaria") and across the world?

I thank God that a youth ministry that had a vision, not just for their immediate community, but for the entire city, reached "across the tracks" to share the goods news with my family. Their vision was bold, and as a result, their impact was huge.

It's easy to get myopic about the four walls of your youth room, and forget how big the community and world you live in actually are. Jesus is calling you to have a bold enough vision that you can make an impact far beyond your own walls.

More and more youth leaders I know are getting a heart for the lost teenagers across their cities, and their plans are reflecting this broader vision. These plans are so big that God has to show up, and other youth leaders need to be recruited to help accomplish this vision. (Remember the Kenosha Allies gospel advancing efforts in chapter 1?)

But you need to think globally too. The power of mission trips can give your teenagers a heart for the world like nothing else. Experiencing the mission field will cause them to pray differently, to give differently and to act differently.

In the words of my good friend and missions expert, Dave, "If you have a heart to reach America, you have 5% of God's heart." There are billions of people in the world, many of whom have never heard of Jesus or His good news. A bold vision starts with your community, but it's not fully complete until it begins stretching across oceans.

Developing a bold vision across the street, across the tracks and around the world will trigger miracles you never imagined. Lives will be changed, souls will be saved and tragic situations will be transformed. Your teenagers will never be the same as a result of them joining you in the pursuit of a bold vision for the glory of God!

VALUE #6: BIBLICAL OUTCOMES MEASURE IT.

Outcome is a word that sounds a bit technical and "businesslike." But God is all about outcomes. Outcomes reflect the results of our labors—the fruit that we are seeking to produce as a result of our ministry efforts.

When Barnabas visited Antioch in Acts 11:19-24, he *"saw what the grace of God had done."* What did he see? He saw outcomes! He witnessed firsthand the fruit of the good news being preached and accepted. What did that fruit look like? It was both qualitative and quantitative. In other words, it was good and there was lots of it. In the same way, we want to see the evidence of God blessing our ministry efforts—"outcomes"—on both levels.

On a qualitative level, we want our teenagers to grow in their knowledge of and service to Jesus. As Peter reminded his Jewish friends in 2 Peter 1:5-8:

> *For this very reason, make every effort to add to your faith goodness; and to goodness, knowledge; and to knowledge, self-control; and*

to self-control, perseverance; and to perseverance, godliness; and to godliness, mutual affection; and to mutual affection, love. For if you possess these qualities in increasing measure, they will keep you from being ineffective and unproductive in your knowledge of our Lord Jesus Christ.

God wants our teenagers to develop godly character and be "productive and effective" for His kingdom. These are the qualitative outcomes He is looking for and working toward in them and in us.

On a quantitative level, these outcomes have to do with the number of people we are impacting with the gospel of Jesus. As Acts 2:47 reminds us, *"the Lord added to their number daily those who were being saved."*

This particular value should prompt you to personally ask the tough, but critical, questions. Questions like:

- What percentage of your teenagers are actively sharing their faith with their peers?
- What percentage of your youth group became Christians as a result of your teenagers' outreach efforts?

You see, it's not just about numbers. It's about the **right** numbers. And the right numbers have to do with how many are coming to Christ and growing in Christ, as a result of you mobilizing your teenagers for making disciples who make disciples.

 VALUE #7: ONGOING PROGRAMS REFLECT IT.

In those days when the number of disciples was increasing, the Hellenistic Jews among them complained against the Hebraic Jews because their widows were being overlooked in the daily distribution of food. So the Twelve gathered all the disciples together and said, "It would not be right for us to neglect the

ministry of the word of God in order to wait on tables. Brothers and sisters, choose seven men from among you who are known to be full of the Spirit and wisdom. We will turn this responsibility over to them and will give our attention to prayer and the ministry of the word" (Acts 6:1-4).

The apostles could have gotten caught up in the minutia and micromanaged every aspect of ministry, but they didn't. They delegated some ministry responsibilities, so they could take care of their top ministry priorities.

What were their top priorities? To give their attention *"to prayer and the ministry of the word."* As a matter of fact, if you look closely at what was actually going on in this passage, you'll see evidence that they prioritized these same seven gospel advancing values we're in the process of unpacking! Think of it like this…

Value #1: They programmed prayer.

Value #2: They programmed evangelism, because part of the ministry *"of the word"* is evangelistic in nature.

Value #3: They had built into leaders who reflected these same values, because we see at least two of them prayerfully and passionately preaching the gospel in later chapters—Stephen in chapter seven of Acts and Philip in chapter eight.

Value #4: All of this is a result of the fact that *"the number of disciples was increasing."*

Value #5: This rapid multiplication was an outgrowth of the bold vision Jesus laid out in Acts 1:8.

Value #6: Feeding the poor is definitely a biblical outcome, as is the number of disciples being multiplied

Value #7: Since this is a key passage for programming your priorities, it's hard to miss this one!

As a result of the apostles' relentless commitment to programming their priorities, the early church was a gospel advancing powerhouse. They didn't let other priorities, or other people's priorities, hijack the plane. Instead, they delegated other duties to qualified leaders and kept their eye on the end goal.

In the same way, you must program these seven values into your daily schedule, weekly programs and annual calendar. This is the only way they will truly become ministry priorities, because what dominates your schedule dominates you. If you don't purposefully and passionately incorporate these values into your programs and your calendar, they're just words on a wall (or flyer or website).

THE DAY I MADE OUR STAFF CRINGE

I'll never forget the day some of the key members of our Dare 2 Share staff took a tour of a large, evangelical ministry. Our two ministries were courting each other for a possible partnership, and they wanted us to know what their ministry was all about from top to bottom.

As we stopped at their value station, they shared with us the many values that drove them organizationally. I noticed that evangelism was at the top of the list. I raised my hand and asked the tour guide, "Where is evangelism programmed into your ministry?" She stopped and looked at me for a moment with her mouth open. It was then I noticed the "abort" look in the eyes of my staff members. But I was already knee-deep in the awkward moment, so I thought it was time to go deeper. I forged ahead and said, "Well, you told us how many different divisions and ministries you have around here, which ones are devoted primarily to evangelism, since it's your top value?"

She didn't have an answer, because there was none and, at the time, the value of evangelism was not marinated deeply into the meat of any of the programs represented there.

But that knee-deep awkward moment needs to be relived in every foyer of every church and on every website of every youth group where there's a slogan or mission statement that reads something like: "To know Him and make Him known."

If it's not programmed, it's a pipedream, not a priority. If it is programmed, then it is a priority that will pipe in reality to that dream through God's strength.

TIME TO GET COOKIN'

These seven values are the seven basic ingredients needed to build a Gospel Advancing Ministry. Remember, the basic ingredients are the same, but how you mix and match them into a spicy new dish is up to you. You can make a taco, burrito, tostada or whatever recipe best fits your taste and context.

As you begin to stir these values into your ministry, you and your teenagers will *taste and see that the Lord is good.*

And so is Mexican food, by the way.

SPICE IT UP...

Questions to help you and your leaders "Gospelize *YOUR* Youth Ministry."

1. What did you think of Greg's Mexican food illustration?

2. When you take an honest look at our youth ministry program, which of the seven ingredients/values of a Gospel Advancing Ministry are we doing the best job incorporating? Which one are we the weakest at?

3. What's one thing we could try right away that might help us make prayer a higher priority in our ministry efforts?

4. Do you think our students know how to relationally share their faith and explain the message of the gospel?

5. Is sharing your faith a priority in your own personal life? Why or why not?

6. How effective do you think our youth ministry currently is at making disciples who make disciples?

7. How would you articulate the vision for our youth ministry?

8. When it comes to qualitative biblical outcomes, how do you think we're doing at helping our teenagers grow in their knowledge of and service to Jesus?

9. When it comes to quantitative biblical outcomes, what percentage of our youth group became Christians as a result of our teenagers' outreach efforts?

10. On a scale of one to ten, how effective do you think we presently are at programming our priorities into our weekly meetings? What's one thing we could try right away that might help us better incorporate this value?

CHAPTER 04

PRAY FIRST

GOSPEL ADVANCING MINISTRY VALUE #1
Intercessory prayer fuels it.

At the outset of the first Gulf War known as Operation Desert Storm, four-star US Army General Norman Schwarzkopf began an air assault against Iraq that obliterated the Saddam Hussein-inspired defiance of the Iraqi forces. Over the course of roughly 40 days, Schwarzkopf dispatched coalition planes on 100,000 missions, dropping some 85,000 tons of bombs over key targets all across Iraq.[1]

During those 40 days, the bombardment destroyed the morale and determination of the

Iraqi army. By the time the ground troops came in, Iraqi soldiers were surrendering to the CNN crews who were there to capture footage.

By battle standards, the actual Gulf War ground invasion was anticlimactic. The war had been won long before the first grunt put his boot on the rubble-strewn streets of Bagdad.

The battle had been won in the air.

The same is true when it comes to advancing the gospel in and through your teenagers. As a youth leader, when you choose to invade Satan's turf and rescue teen captives from his grip by moving Jesus' message of grace deeply into their lives, you are stepping onto the battlefield. Your opponent in this fight is the most powerful created being in the universe. Satan, and his well organized army of unholy terrorists, won't go down without a fight, and hand-to-hand combat with them is a gritty, bloody prospect.

That's why you must call in air support. For it's only through prayer that you can call in the missiles of God's power from heaven to obliterate the enemy's strongholds over your teenagers, schools and community.

This is exactly what the early church did. This is exactly why they won the battle for advancing the gospel from Jerusalem to the ends of the earth.

It only takes a cursory reading of the book of Acts to see that prayer was the engine of every move the early believers made. Their "pray first" philosophy drove their strategy, problem solving, group meetings and disciple multiplication efforts.

They prayed first...

> ...when they were waiting for the promised Holy Spirit.
> *They all joined together constantly in prayer...*
> (Acts 1:14).

...when they were making key leadership decisions.

> *Then they prayed, "Lord, you know everyone's heart.*
> *Show us which of these two you have chosen..."*
> (Acts 1:24).

...when they kicked off the first official church services.

> *They devoted themselves to the apostles' teaching and to*
> *the fellowship, to the breaking of bread and to prayer...*
> (Acts 2:42).

...when they were threatened and told to stop evangelizing.

> *On their release, Peter and John went back to their own*
> *people and reported all that the chief priests and the*
> *elders had said to them. When they heard this, they*
> *raised their voices together in prayer to God*
> (Acts 4:23-24).

...when they decided what their key leadership priorities should be.

> *"We...will give our attention to prayer and the ministry*
> *of the word" (Acts 6:4).*

...when they faced hardships, like Peter being thrown in prison.

> *...but the church was earnestly praying to God*
> (Acts 12:5).

...when they sent out their first official missionaries.

> *So after they had fasted and prayed, they placed their*
> *hands on them and sent them off (Acts 13:3).*

...when they selected leaders for the new church plants.

> *Paul and Barnabas appointed elders for them in*
> *each church and, with prayer and fasting, committed*
> *them to the LORD, in whom they had put their trust*
> (Acts 14:23).

And on, and on, and on, it goes. A "pray first" philosophy permeated the whole of the early church. From the first page to the last, the stories in the book of Acts drip with intercession. So should the story of your youth ministry.

In his final book to his younger protégé, Timothy, Paul reiterates the number one priority in programming the church services Timothy was overseeing:

> I urge, then, first of all, that requests, prayers, intercession and thanksgiving be made for everyone—for kings and all those in authority, that we may live peaceful and quiet lives in all godliness and holiness. This is good, and pleases God our Savior, who wants all men to be saved and to come to a knowledge of the truth (1 Timothy 2:1-4).

Paul is reminding Timothy that the first order of business is not business, not music, not even the sermon. Priority **numero uno** is prayer—all kinds of prayers, for all kinds of people. What's true of the church service is true of your youth group meeting.

With this as a backdrop, here are a few questions to wrestle with when it comes to prayer:

- When you begin a leadership team meeting, do you spend enough quality time in prayer to ensure that you are getting your direction from on high?

- Are you more inclined to run to your whiteboard to write out your ministry strategy, or to run to your prayer closet to discover God's strategy first?

- Is prayer programmed into your youth group meetings and small group gatherings on a consistent basis?

- Do you have a personal rhythm of prayer that keeps your prayer life fresh and powerful on a consistent basis?

- Do your teenagers know how to pray? Have you taught them? Are you modeling it for them?

JUST WHAT IS INTERCESSORY PRAYER?

The primary type of prayer Paul was challenging Timothy to build into the church services in this passage was intercessory prayer. Intercession is simply a big word for praying to God on behalf of other people's needs.

These needs may be physical, financial, emotional or relational in nature. But given the context of this passage, it seems like Paul is specifically referring to praying on behalf of other's deep spiritual needs. This type of prayer leans heavily into praying for believers to grow deeply in their faith, love and spiritual maturity. Paul provides us with a vivid example of this in Philippians 1:9-11:

> And this is my prayer: that your love may abound more and more in knowledge and depth of insight, so that you may be able to discern what is best and may be pure and blameless until the day of Christ, filled with the fruit of righteousness that comes through Jesus.

Intercessory prayer also challenges believers to pray for each other about fearlessly sharing the good news of Jesus. One of my favorite passages in the book of Ephesians is:

> Pray also for me, that whenever I open my mouth, words may be given me so that I will fearlessly make known the mystery of the gospel, for which I am an ambassador in chains. Pray that I may declare it fearlessly, as I should (Ephesians 6:19-20).

Isn't it refreshing to know that the great Apostle Paul needed others to pray for him to be bold when sharing the gospel? Paul depended on the intercessory prayers of other believers to infuse him with divine fearlessness to gospelize the Gentiles!

In the same way, you need to pray for your teenagers to grow deep in their faith, as they fearlessly go wide with the Jesus' message of grace. It is this kind of intercessory prayer that will pave the way as your teenagers accelerate toward living and giving the good news throughout their spheres of influence with increasing momentum.

Another interesting aspect of Paul's instructions to Timothy about prioritizing prayer in the church services is its focus on the lost. Paul tells Timothy to pray specifically for everyone from kings and leaders to everyday Joes and Jennas to be transformed by the good news of Jesus Christ.

Because there were no church buildings during this era, most believers met in homes. Imagine times of focused prayer where the souls of friends, family members, coworkers, neighbors and even government leaders were passionately and relentlessly lifted up to the throne of God. No wonder so many people came to faith in Christ in the 1st century! They insistently and incessantly tapped into the golden key that unlocks the salvific power of God through the prayers of His people.

PRAY FIRST

What if that was the pattern in your youth group meetings and small group gatherings? What if "first of all" prayers were poured out for the souls of the lost? I'm convinced from both biblical evidence and personal experience that your youth ministry would explode with new conversion growth.

God has a heart for the teenagers in your community—a bigger heart than even you have! He *desires all men to be saved and to come to a knowledge of the truth.* So when you engage in prayer for the lost, you tap into the mighty river of compassion, mercy and love that flow through His divine veins, and a transfusion takes place in your heart and in the hearts of your teenagers. Soon the very heart of your youth ministry will be beating and bleeding for the lost in rhythm with His.

Does this brand of intercession pulse through your youth group, your leadership team meetings and your own personal prayer life? If not, what will it take to get there?

Sadly, the average church service today spends more time making announcements than engaging in intercessory prayer. If prayer is focused on at all in the typical church or youth group, there's often a tendency to relegate, delegate and abdicate the responsibility to a small group of "intercessors"—who, for whatever reason, tend to be wide-eyed, twitchy and appear to be ultra-caffeinated.

It was Jesus Himself who created a "pray first" template for transformation in Mark 1:35-39:

> *Very early in the morning, while it was still dark, Jesus got up, left the house and went off to a solitary place, where he prayed. Simon and his companions went to look for him, and when they found him, they exclaimed: "Everyone is looking for you!" Jesus replied, "Let us go somewhere else—to the nearby villages—so I can preach there also. That is why I have come." So he traveled throughout Galilee, preaching in their synagogues and driving out demons.*

Jesus prayed first. He got away to pray. He would even miss a few ministry opportunities to pray. Jesus needed those times of communion with the Father where He received strength, wisdom and marching orders from on high. As my friend, Dr. Dann Spader, often says, Jesus didn't pull His "God card" out in order to carry out His earthly ministry.[2] He worked out of prayer and in full dependence on the Spirit who dwelt in Him (Matthew 3:17-20). Although He was fully God and fully human, He chose to live as a human who was full of the Spirit of God.

In a similar way, you can, like Jesus, live your life empowered by the Spirit for the mission He has given you...and so can your teenagers! But in order for this to happen, prayer must characterize your life and ministry!

As a result of Jesus' "pray first" philosophy, eventually thousands of Jews across Jerusalem, Judea, Samaria and Galilee were transformed by the gospel! This Spirit-empowered, radical rabbi set the pattern for the early church to follow. And follow it they did!

 #GOSPELIZE *Sadly, the average church service today spends more time making announcements than engaging in intercessory prayer.*

In Acts 4, when Peter and John were threatened by the Sanhedrin—the same crew that demanded Jesus be crucified—and were told to keep quiet about Jesus, they reported back to the church what had happened. What was their first reaction? Did they make a plan? Did they launch a research committee? Did they run away? No!

They prayed first! They prayed for God to demonstrate His power and give them Holy Spirit boldness to proclaim the message of Jesus! And God answered in an earth-rattling way.

Acts 4:31 captures this clearly: *"After they prayed, the place where they were meeting was shaken. And they were all filled with the Holy Spirit and spoke the word of God boldly."* This one verse recounts the DNA of Jesus being infused into the early church by the Holy Spirit. It clearly paints a pattern for revival which your youth group can emulate. This pattern starts with prayer, culminates with proclamation and shakes everything up along the way!

Here's how their "pray first" philosophy shook things up 2,000 years ago:

1. The building was shaken with the power of prayer.

2. The believers were shaken with the power of the Spirit.

3. The city was shaken with the power of the gospel.

Let's break these three down further, and consider what it might look like to apply them to your youth ministry context.

SHAKEN WITH THE POWER OF PRAYER

First of all, the building was shaken with the power of prayer. Imagine the scene. Peter and John had just recently been miraculously released from the threats of the Sanhedrin—the same group of Jewish leaders who'd initiated the crucifixion of Jesus. When Peter and John share this miraculous news with the believers, they all lift their voices to God and pray in Holy Spirit-orchestrated unity:

> Sovereign Lord," they said, "you made the heavens and the earth and the sea, and everything in them...Now, Lord, consider their threats and enable your servants to speak your word with great boldness" (Acts 4:24b,29).

God's "Amen" to their prayer triggered an earthquake under their feet. The building was literally shaken by the power of prayer.

I believe that the secret to their collective prayers' dramatic impact was that they didn't pray for deliverance. Instead, they prayed for boldness to proclaim the good news of Jesus to an antagonistic audience. These believers knew that this prayer could end with their heads on a pike and their bodies in a grave, but they were willing to pay the price of being a witness for the Lord Jesus.

In our pluralistic society, where Jesus is fine and good until you say He's the only way to heaven, your teenagers may not lose their lives, but they could lose their cool. Their popularity could plummet, and their friends could flee. Prayer will give your teenagers the evangelistic boldness and power they need to speak the truth in love to a potentially antagonistic audience. Prayer will also prepare the hearts of their peers to hear and accept the gospel message. As someone once said, "We must talk to God about people, before we talk to people about God."

What about Bob?

I'll never forget when the "building was shaken" by the power of prayer for me personally. It was roughly fifteen years ago. I was attending my first Youth Ministry Executive Council meeting in Washington, D.C.

Bob was loud, winsome and well-dressed. His hair was perfectly combed as he came bursting into this room full of other national youth ministry leaders. Initially, he struck me as part Elvis, part Pentecostal preacher and part used car salesman.

This group of ministry leaders was gathered at this national meeting to strategize about reaching every teenager in the nation for Jesus Christ. There were leading representatives from almost every major denomination and youth-focused, para-church organization in America. From conservative, to mainline, to charismatic, all sorts of leaders were there representing a plethora of ministries. But we all gathered with one heart—to reach the youth of our nation with the gospel of Jesus Christ.

Bob was all in. Over the few days we were there, you couldn't help but feel Bob's absolute resonance with the mission. From hearty "amen's," to slaps on the back, you'd have known where Bob was in the meeting room even if you'd been blindfolded.

Then it happened. We broke up into groups and prayed, and somehow, I got stuck at the Pentecostal table. And Bob was leading the band wagon.

Now, you have to understand that I was saved in a Baptist church, and raised in a Bible church, so I didn't quite know how to keep up with Bob and crew. They were naming and claiming, while I was sitting and cringing. Every once in awhile, I'd throw in a "Make it so, Lord," to try to keep up.

Bob started in a clockwise circle, and loudly proceeded around the circle one by one asking, "What's your prayer request, son?" I was the last one in the circle.

One by one, my Pentecostal brothers uttered their bold request, and one by one, Bob prayed over them with an intensity that made me feel like I was sitting in a windy upper room with the original apostles.

During this process, I could tell that the other prayer circles of various denominations and organizations were leaning in and listening to the prayers at our table, because our group was dominating the room. The Baptists' "Amens" and the para-church leaders' chatter paled before the intercessions of Bob.

Then the big hand of the clockwise prayers stopped on me. Bob looked at me with a prophet's piercing eyes and hollered, "And what's your prayer request, son?"

My mind scrambled. I thought to myself, 'They've all been praying for their ministries, and getting louder and louder. Maybe if I pray for something personal, it will calm them—a.k.a. Bob—down. Without thinking I blurted, "Pray for my wife and me to have kids. We've been married for about ten years, and still haven't had any children!"

That was like chumming a shark tank. Bob jumped up and yelled, "I've prayed for hundreds of couples, and they've never failed to have kids. Gather round, boys!"

"Oh no. Oh no! Oh no!!!" I thought.

Oh, yes.

They gathered around me, in the middle of this group of national youth ministry leaders, and placed their hands on my head. Then Bob began to call out to God—in front of God and everyone. I'm sure these weren't the exact words, but it went something like…"Dear God, I pray right now you touch this man's SPERM and bring it to life! And touch his wife's eggs, and bring them together in a holy collision of life and love! And give them a baby, in the name of Jesus!!!!"

Bob prayed for what seemed like hours—it was probably only 2 minutes—as the whole room leaned in, and I cringed in utter embarrassment. When he finished with his prayer, he looked at me with his crazy eyes and boldly proclaimed, "It is done! It is done, in the name of Jesus!"

To which I said something like, "It ain't quite done yet, because faith without works is dead!" The laughter around the prayer circle and around the room broke the awkward moment, but I think my face was red for the rest of the night.

And three weeks later my wife got pregnant.

We found out two months later, and traced it back.

Bada bing.

I sent Bob a postcard that read, "Dear Bob, IT IS DONE! My wife is pregnant! Thanks for your prayer!"

Now, Bob and I may still differ a bit on some of the finer points of theology, but I tell you what, Bob prayed like God was standing right there and I, up to that point, prayed like a wuss.

Now, every time I look at my teenage son, and his younger sister, who I jokingly call "The Second Blessing," I'm reminded of the power of intercessory prayer.

I know that God doesn't answer every prayer with a "yes." I also understand that suffering is part of God forging and forming us into the image of His dear Son. But I also believe that we don't see a lot of things happen in our lives and ministries, because we don't really believe that prayer works like that.

Some preachers have even watered their prayer theology down enough to say, "The only thing prayer changes is us."

That's a crock. Of course, prayer changes us. It makes us more dependent on Him, and less dependent on our own abilities. It causes us to empty ourselves, so that He can fill us and fuel us. But even a cursory reading of the Bible makes it clear that prayer unleashes the sovereignty of God to transform human events.

Moses prayed like prayer changed situations.

So did David.

So did Nehemiah.

So did Daniel.

So did Jesus.

So did His followers—see the book of Acts.

If the power of God is the water, then prayer is the spigot that releases it. God, in His sovereignty, has chosen that He will often change given situations as a direct result of prayer. When He says, "No," He's got a better answer for us than "Yes!" As Jesus said in Matthew 7:9-11:

> *"Which of you, if your son asks for bread, will give him a stone? Or if he asks for a fish, will give him a snake? If you, then, though you are evil, know how to give good gifts to your children, how much more will your Father in heaven give good gifts to those who ask him!"*

God loves to give good gifts **to** His kids! And intercessory prayer is how God gives good gifts **through** His kids, just like God used Bob to give my wife and me a great gift when he prayed his blush-inducing prayer on our behalf.

That night in Washington, D.C., the building was shaken with the power of prayer for me. Although I am still theologically conservative in the broad spectrum of Christianity, I began to learn to pray with faith and boldness from Bob that night—or to be totally honest, that day we saw the two blue stripes on the pregnancy test! God began to do a work in my heart that would forever change the way I view and do youth ministry.

God has given you the same privilege and opportunity in your youth group. You can collectively go straight to the King of kings and Lord of lords to present your requests to Him. You can intercede on behalf of the lost and each other. You can ask Him to provide for your "daily bread" and personal requests, and He WILL answer. Although He doesn't always answer with a "Yes," He always answers with what's best!

SHAKEN WITH THE POWER OF THE SPIRIT

Consider again the sequence of events in Acts 4:31: *"After they prayed, the place where they were meeting was shaken. And they were all filled with the Holy Spirit..."*

Prayer is the portal through which we yield ourselves to the power of the Holy Spirit. The act of prayer is an act of dependence. Prayer is us letting God know that we can't, but we believe He can. It's how we stay connected to the Vine, because apart from Him we *"can do nothing"* (John 15:5).

I almost lost the ministry I lead—Dare 2 Share—before I fully realized this. In 2008, when "The Great Recession" punched

America's economy in the face, a lot of ministries were knocked to their knees, including us.

Because our ministry is heavily dependent on donations, we were hit hard. We lost half of our donated income. We had to cut back from 48 employees to 23. Our bank account was depleted to almost nothing and our reserves were gone.

That's when my prayer life really kicked into high gear. I knew that unless God intervened, the ministry could be completely lost.

And slowly, but surely, we began to see God answer prayers in miraculous ways. The Lord came through again and again and rescued us from financial collapse.

Something strange happened in the process. I began to get hooked on prayer. I began to realize that it was through prayer that God not only provided finances for our ministry, but strength for my soul. Soon prayer walks became a regular part of my routine. During these times, I would pray for the lost to be reached, for believers to grow deeper in their faith, for needs to be met, but also for divine power to fuel me during the week. Prayer is how I began to get filled with the Spirit, so that I could be fueled for the mission He put in front of me.

I recently visited Israel for the first time and was blown away by the proximity between where Jesus most likely had the Passover meal with His disciples and His walk to the Garden of Gethsemane where He would be arrested. He made time on this short walk between these two significant places to give His disciples their final lesson before He would be arrested, beaten and crucified. It was a lesson on dependency on Him and reliance on the Holy Spirit:

> *"I am the true vine, and my Father is the gardener. He cuts off every branch in me that bears no fruit, while every branch that does bear fruit he prunes so that it will be even more fruitful.*

You are already clean because of the word I have spoken to you. Remain in me, and I will remain in you. No branch can bear fruit by itself; it must remain in the vine. Neither can you bear fruit unless you remain in me. I am the vine; you are the branches. If a man remains in me and I in him, he will bear much fruit; apart from me you can do nothing" (John 15:1-5).

John 14-17 contains some of the most powerful lessons on prayer, faith and the Holy Spirit in the whole of Scripture. It was His final sermon to His beloved disciples before He was crushed for our transgressions. In that sermon He reminded them of the priority of prayerful dependence on Him.

In the same way you and your teenagers can stay connected to the vine through faith-filled, relentless prayer. It took a resurrection for the disciples to begin to realize that. It took a recession for me to begin to realize that. But please, don't wait for a disaster. Learn from my mistakes, and start connecting to the branch now. And get your teenagers to follow your lead. When you do, here's what Jesus promises: *"If you remain in me and my words remain in you, ask whatever you wish, and it will be given you"* (John 15:7).

As we are filled with the Holy Spirit through prayer, our requests will be answered through prayer. We will witness true miracles and especially the miracle of changed lives! When our teenagers get a taste of the power of God working in them and through them, it will reinforce how essential it is that they stay connected to the vine.

SHAKEN BY THE POWER OF THE GOSPEL

"After they prayed, the place where they were meeting was shaken. And they were all filled with the Holy Spirit and spoke the word of God boldly" (Acts 4:31).

Once the early believers were fueled by prayer and filled by the Spirit, they were ready to fearlessly spread the gospel! Why? Because the Spirit always desires to testify about Jesus, and when you are truly controlled by Him, you can't help but point others to the Son of God! As Jesus told His disciples in John 15: 26-27:

"When the Counselor comes, whom I will send to you from the Father, the Spirit of truth who goes out from the Father, he will testify about me. And you also must testify, for you have been with me from the beginning."

How does the Holy Spirit testify about Jesus? Through your lips! Think about the first thing the disciples did when they were baptized by the Holy Spirit on the day of Pentecost. They testified about who Jesus was! Their tongues were set on fire by the Holy Spirit, and they testified to the fact that *"God has made this Jesus, whom you crucified, both Lord and Christ"* (Acts 2:36).

When someone tells me that they seek to live a life full of the Spirit, but they don't ever share the good news of Jesus, I have a hard time believing them. If you are full of the Holy Spirit, you won't be able to contain your evangelistic efforts, and neither will your teenagers!

TEN SACRED MINUTES

A few years back, when I was speaking at a youth leader training session in Chicago, I riffed about the lack of priority youth ministry puts on intercessory prayer. A hand went up in the audience and a particular youth leader shared that he, too, had been convicted by the Holy Spirit that prayer should be a bigger part of his youth ministry focus. So he decided to do something about it. He actually made prayer a significant part of his weekly youth ministry meetings.

He dedicated the last ten minutes of his Wednesday night meetings to intercessory prayer. Getting his students in a big circle each week, they began to pray for the Holy Spirit to fill them and fuel

GOSPEL ADVANCING STORIES FROM THE FRONT LINES
By John Curiale

The first step in creating a Gospel Advancing Ministry is to lay the foundation. And that foundation is prayer. In 1 Timothy 2:1-4, before Paul tells Timothy any of the qualifications for elders, he tells them to pray.

One of the reasons why we pray is so our hearts align with His heart. And His heart is that nobody perishes. His heart is that everyone would come to know Him.

When I started as a youth pastor, I struggled like any youth pastor. Sometimes you're just showing up, and you're like, I don't even really love these people, you know?

I'm just being honest...

But through prayer, God got me on my knees, and gave me His compassion, and so my heart was aligning with His through prayer.

As I prayed, my heart broke—kind of like when Jesus went down the mountain and He looked on the crowd and saw all these people that were lost without a shepherd. He had compassion. That was the first mark of His ministry. That is why He came—to seek and save the lost.

So I started to spend my Thursdays with my note cards that had the name of every single student in my group. I would pray for two hours. After that God starting growing the ministry.

I learned that prayer empowers us to really love what God loves—which is for all to come to know Him. And it empowers us to hate what God hates—which is for people not to come to know Him. Prayer is like a catalyst for evangelism. It compels us to go out. And because the ground is softened through prayer, more will come to know Him. Then after people know Him, discipleship happens, and those students begin to get trained to share the gospel, as well.

them for evangelism during the coming week. They prayed that God would prepare the hearts of their classmates for the gospel, and that He would open up opportunities to share Jesus with them.

This youth leader admitted that, at first, this mandatory prayer time was awkward. There would be long periods of silence from time to time. But he kept doing it week after week, and finally, the teenagers began to catch on.

He went on to tell the room full of youth leaders that this prayer time was now the part of the weekly youth group time that his teenagers looked forward to the most. Not the games, not the Bible lesson, but prayer. It was this consistent intercessory prayer focus that enlarged the hearts of his teenagers toward evangelism, opened up opportunities for gospel conversations and prepared the hearts of their peers for the gospel.

May you, like the church in Acts 4:31, be truly shaken by the power of prayer, and shake your city with the gospel as a result!

So what level of "air control" do you have?

Remember the opening illustration of this chapter about the Gulf War, and how it was the coalition forces' air supremacy that led to a decisive victory. Did you know that there are actually three terms used to describe the levels of control an air force has in a battle situation?

The first is called "air parity." This simply means that one air force controls the air space over its own soldiers on a particular battlefield. This is the minimum level of control that an army needs to protect its soldiers from harm, because it makes it possible to take out enemy soldiers who are making their way across the battle line.

The second level of control is "air superiority." This simply means that the air space over the entire battlefield is primarily controlled by one's own army. Overall, the battle for the air space is generally being won by your army.

Finally, there is "air supremacy." This represents an army's complete control of the airspace over the entire battlefield. Once air supremacy is established by one side, it becomes next to impossible for the opposing force to win.

You and your youth group are in a battle with Satan for the advancement of the gospel in and through your teenagers. He has captured the battlefield and taken the broken lives of the unreached young people in your city captive. What level of air control do you have over the battlefield in your city?

Do you have air supremacy? Are you and your teenagers covering your group and your community in prayer? Are you and your teenagers relentlessly interceding with God on behalf of their unreached friends, classmates, teammates and family members? At this level of prayer, intercession is consistent and persistent. It has permeated the entire culture of your youth ministry efforts.

Or maybe you've established air superiority. Perhaps you've gained momentum, and praying for each other and the lost is becoming a bigger and bigger priority in your personal life and ministry programming. You know you have a ways to go, but you feel more and more excited about the direction you are leading your teenagers in conversing with their heavenly Father about the souls of their lost friends.

Or perhaps you're only at air parity. You basically control the "air space" over your teenagers, and spend most of your time praying over their spiritual and emotional needs. While that's a necessary and important step, it's not nearly enough if you are going to truly see momentum in this vitally important area of ministry.

Sadly, some of you may be reading this and realize that you have no "air control" at all. For you, prayer is merely the "holy water" you use to sprinkle on your whiteboard strategies, or the necessary ritual every Christian uses to begin meetings.

But it's never too late. It took me forty-two years of my life and a ministry financial crisis to really amp up my prayer life. But I'm so glad it has become a bigger and bigger priority.

In the words of E.M. Bounds in his book, *Power Through Prayer*:

> What the Church needs today is not more machinery or better, not new organizations or more and novel methods, but men whom the Holy Ghost can use—men of prayer, men mighty in prayer. The Holy Ghost does not flow through methods, but through men. He does not come on machinery, but on men. He does not anoint plans, but men—men of prayer.[3]

May you become mighty in prayer, and lead your teenagers to do the same!

SPICE IT UP...

Questions to help you and your leaders "Gospelize _YOUR_ Youth Ministry."

1. Do you **really** believe that prayer changes situations?

2. Have you ever personally seen a miraculous answer to intercessory prayer?

3. Are you personally more inclined to run to your list of things to do in the course of your day, or to run to prayer?

4. What are some ways you could adjust your personal rhythm of prayer so that your prayer life stays fresh and powerful on a consistent basis?

5. Which one best describes our youth ministry in the area of prayer—air parity, air superiority or air supremacy?

6. When we begin a leadership team meeting do we spend enough quality time in prayer to ensure that we are getting our direction from on high?

7. How could we as leaders be praying more effectively for individual students in our ministry?

8. Do our teenagers know how to pray? Have we taught them? Are we, as leaders, modeling it for them?

9. How could we better program prayer into our youth group meetings and small group gatherings on a consistent basis?

10. Spend some serious time praying together for your ministry.

CHAPTER 05

START IN YOUR CIRCLE

GOSPEL ADVANCING MINISTRY VALUE #2
Relational evangelism drives it.

Think about how many "friends" the average teenager in your youth group has. Instagram + Facebook + Twitter + Classmates + Teammates + Neighborhood Friends = A Whole Heck of a Lot! Then think about how many of these friends would never dream of darkening the doors of a church.

Simply put, the best possible means of advancing the gospel to this generation is by motivating and mobilizing your teenagers to share Jesus in their circles of relationship. Your living, breathing, Christian teenagers going about their daily lives are themselves the best outreach strategy possible. Check out the Apostle Paul's perspective on this:

> *You yourselves are our letter, written on our hearts, known and read by everybody. You show that you are a letter from Christ, the result of our ministry, written not with ink but with the Spirit of the living God, not on tablets of stone but on tablets of human hearts* (2 Corinthians 3:2-3).

Your teens are a letter from Christ, known and read by everybody. And when you inspire and equip them to share the gospel with their friends, they become a walking, talking, loving, relational, personalized "outreach meeting" everywhere they go!

Done well, nothing can be more organic, authentic, impacting and viral than friend-to-friend sharing. If you look closely throughout the book of Acts, you'll discover a riptide of gospel conversations happening friend to friend and family member to family member all across the ancient world. This person-to-person gospel advancing movement doesn't always grab our attention like the tongues-on-fire disciples gathering a curious crowd in Acts 2, or like Paul's preaching on Mar's Hill. But in the long run, I'm convinced that it did more to spread the Word to the world than all 12 apostles—even with Paul thrown in for good measure!

Yet even Paul, dynamic preacher that he was, understood the power of relational evangelism. Consider his words in Acts 16:31, where he tells the post-earthquake-terrified Philippian jailer: *"Believe in the Lord Jesus, and you will be saved—you and your household."* Paul knew that once the family patriarch came to Jesus, the rest of his family members, servants and friends would fall like Holy Spirit tipped dominoes.

Or consider Acts 18:8: *"Crispus, the synagogue leader, and his entire household believed in the Lord; and many of the Corinthians who heard Paul believed and were baptized."*

In the Greek, the word household—*oikos*—is much broader than just your immediate family members. Michael Green, in his book *Evangelism in the Early Church,* explains the strategic implications of this as follows:

> The family, understood in this broad way as consisting of blood relations, slaves, clients and friends, was one of the bastions of Graeco-Roman society. Christian missionaries made a deliberate point of gaining whatever households they could as lighthouses, so to speak, from which the gospel could illuminate the surrounding darkness.[1]

REACHING YOUR *OIKOS*

This is exactly how my family—and many of our friends, coworkers, neighbors and more—came to Jesus. As I mentioned in the Introduction, my Uncle Jack trusted in Jesus, then told his coworker and fellow bodybuilder, Thumper, about Jesus. As soon as Thumper trusted in Jesus, he invited Jack to tell his family members about the good news. Within a few weeks, they'd all put their faith in Jesus and began telling others.

Eventually my uncles Bob, Dave, Tommy and Richard—and their circles—came to faith in Christ. I witnessed all of this firsthand. So I carried the tradition into my neighborhood with my friends. Because my youth leaders equipped me to share my faith, I knew how to share Jesus from takeoff to touchdown. So that's what I did.

As a result, I reached my own circle of neighborhood friends.

Who's in your teenagers' circles?

Each of your teenagers has their own version of an *oikos*, and it is much larger than anyone had in the early church. Their *oikos* is comprised of friends—both online and face-to-face—as well as classmates, teammates, coworkers, family members and more.

Whereas the average person in the New Testament probably had an *oikos* of 8-15 people,[2] the average teenager has a circle of influence that numbers in the hundreds.

If your teenagers can be equipped to engage their family members at home, their peers at school and their friends online, they can take the gospel further, faster than anybody in the book of Acts could have ever dreamed.

As you equip your students for this kind of relational evangelism, you'll need to increasingly relinquish the role of the "quarterback" and take on the role of a coach. Let me explain.

In the typical youth ministry, the youth leader is the quarterback of evangelism. In this mindset, invitational evangelism is the game plan. The youth leader actively encourages teenagers to bring their friends to an outreach meeting where he/she throws the touchdown pass by giving the gospel and providing an opportunity for students to trust in Christ.

While I'm all for outreach meetings and giving the gospel weekly in your regular meetings, I encourage you to shift your evangelism paradigm from quarterback to coach. You're no longer primarily out front scoring the "conversion points." You're getting your students off the bench and into the game. You're coaching them through the basic skills they need to navigate a gospel conversation, helping them understand strategy, supporting them when they try and fail and celebrating their successes.

In this coaching model, the youth group grows both spiritually and numerically. Sure, as a youth leader you're still pulling off outreach meetings, but your teenagers themselves are engaging their peers before and after those meetings with the claims of Christ.

While there are many methods and tactics for coaching your students on the "how to's" of reaching their friends who need Jesus, there is one basic process that jumps off the pages of the New

Testament again and again. That process is to pray with passion, pursue with love and persuade with truth. At Dare 2 Share, we structure our entire week-long evangelism and leadership summer training events around the "Pray – Pursue – Persuade" evangelism approach, because we believe that this relational strategy is core to effective discipleship multiplication. Let's take a closer look at each part of this simple strategy that can help your teenagers become more purposeful and effective at relationally sharing their faith.

PRAY WITH PASSION

When you inspire your teenagers to begin to pray for their unreached peers, their hearts become more and more in tune with God's. They start to notice the opportunities that God opens every day to engage their friends in spiritual conversations. The Lord breaks down strongholds, both in the hearts of your teenagers that are keeping them from sharing the good news, and in the hearts of their friends that keep them from putting their faith in Jesus. But it all starts with prayer.

Paul writes in Romans, *"Brothers and sisters, my heart's desire and prayer to God for the Israelites is that they may be saved"* (Romans 10:1). Although the Apostle Paul was technically "the apostle to the Gentiles," he had a deep burden on his heart for the people of Israel. He prayed passionately for them to be saved. This great apostle knew that only God could crack the code on their hardened hearts and transform them from the inside out.

In the same way, you must work to create a longing in your students' hearts for their peers and loved ones to be transformed by Jesus. This passionate longing for the lost will trigger relentless prayers in their souls to God on behalf of their unreached friends and family. Let me give you a personal example from when I was a teenager.

Uncle Richard

Growing up, I never really knew my Uncle Richard very well. I just knew that he had moved to Phoenix, Arizona, as a young man to make his fortune in business. And that's exactly what he'd done.

He, like all my other uncles, was tough as nails. I had heard the stories of the fights that he'd been in. Once he'd jumped through the passenger side window of a moving car full of tough guys who were out to get him and his brothers. He took all of them on, as the car wove back and forth down the road for two or three blocks.

After most of my uncles had come to Christ, they began to pray for Richard to become a Christian as well. But whenever they would bring it up, he would stop them cold in their tracks. He didn't want to talk about it.

Then disaster struck our family. Grandpa died of a sudden, massive heart attack. Uncle Richard flew up from Phoenix to be with all of us at the funeral.

I was invited to give the gospel at Grandpa's funeral. I was fifteen years old at the time. Hundreds had crammed into the tiny mortuary as the funeral service began. My mind was reeling and my heart was racing. This was the biggest crowd I had ever spoken in front of before. I knew there were people in the audience that needed to hear the gospel. In spite of the hundreds before me, there was only one person on my mind—Uncle Richard. I knew that he didn't know Christ. I knew that this was a crucial opportunity for him to come to Christ.

The best that I knew how, I shared the gospel and gave an invitation for people to respond. Many did. Uncle Richard didn't. My family was crushed, because of the dual loss—the loss of Grandpa and the loss of Richard's soul.

Soon after the funeral, I wrote a letter to Uncle Richard that expressed how much I prayed that he would become a Christian.

I sent it in hopes that I would soon get word of his salvation. He never responded to my letter. Not a phone call. Not a postcard. Nothing.

I had tried. My uncles had tried. We were at the end of our ropes.

So we prayed. We prayed with passion. We prayed relentlessly. It was out of our hands. It had always been out of our hands, but now we knew it. We felt it. We knew that it would take an act of God to save his hardened soul.

Years went by, but we never stopped praying. Then unexpectedly Uncle Richard was coming into town again for another funeral of sorts...his own. He had melanoma. This deadly cancer had spread throughout his whole body. He flew back to have one last family reunion, and say goodbye to those he loved.

But we wanted to see him again. We wanted to see him in heaven. Still, he made it clear that he didn't want to talk about it. Uncle Bob gave him a letter that told him how much he meant to him, and that he wanted to see him in heaven someday. Richard cried when he read the letter, but refused to talk about death, or heaven, or "religion" or anything of a spiritual nature. In one final last ditch effort, my Uncle Bob talked him into coming to Grace Church the next day with the rest of the family—the church where I was the young, twenty-something, preaching pastor at the time. Uncle Richard was hesitant initially, but finally agreed.

I'll never forget the sight. My uncles, aunts and cousins were crammed into the two last pews. These huge, muscle bound believers had only one thing on their minds—Richard's salvation. They prayed the whole service, because they knew that at the end of my sermon, I would give the gospel.

After painstakingly laying out the message of salvation, I had everybody bow their heads and close their eyes. I then asked for those who had trusted in Christ as their Savior that day to raise their hands. It was something to see. Without a moment's hesitation Richard and his wife, Tarin, thrust their hands into the air. I could hear the sobs of my family. (They had been peeking.) When they saw Richard and Tarin raise their hands, their hearts flooded with uncontainable emotion, and they just couldn't help but cry from pure joy.

Later that day, Richard pulled Bob aside, put his arm around him and said, "Guess what happened, brother? Today I trusted in Jesus Christ. You are going to see me in heaven someday." Bob just wrapped his arms around Richard's frail, cancer-emaciated frame and wept. They said goodbye for the last time on earth, knowing that the next time they would see each other would be in glory.

Richard called later and asked me to give the gospel at his impending memorial service in Arizona. He had been witnessing to his extended family and friends, and he thought that if I gave the gospel at his memorial, then more would have the opportunity to trust in Christ. The last days of his life he was concerned about the lost souls of those around him. He wanted others to hear the good news of salvation through Jesus Christ.

I'm convinced that the years of passionate, persistent prayers of a teenager and a group of body-building brothers (and many others) helped till the soil of Uncle Richard's heart so that he was ready to put his trust in Christ.

PURSUE WITH LOVE

It's interesting to me that the word "love" is nowhere to be found in the book of Acts. But the reality is that it doesn't need to be mentioned, because the acts of love exhibited by the early believers are evident everywhere. Here are just a few examples of their love lived out in sacrificial ways:

- Some sold their property to support those in need (Acts 4:34-35)

- Some willingly crossed taboo racial boundaries to share the good news (Acts 11:19-21).

- Some extended forgiveness to those who were about to kill them (Acts 7:59-60).

The whole book of Acts is a dynamic example of what it looks like to pursue the lost with the love of God from Jerusalem and Judea, to Samaria, to the ends of the earth.

Every gospel conversation was an act of love. It was a risky attempt to connect God's love with humans who had a predisposition to reject it. The early believers took their lives into their own hands every time they shared the good news. But they did it out of love—love for God and love for their others.

Just like Philip literally pursued the Ethiopian's chariot to share the good news with him in Acts 8:26-40, you need to help your teenagers pursue their peers with the love of God. This can come in the form of a listening ear, an encouraging word or a helping hand.

Equipping your teenagers to listen can be especially powerful. There's something magnetic about a teenager who really knows how to ask good questions and listen deeply to others.

Jesus modeled this for us. Throughout the Gospels, He asked hundreds of questions. These questions drew people into deeper discussions, sometimes sparking arguments, and sometimes transforming hearts!

When Jesus asked the Samaritan woman for a drink of water, she was flabbergasted. Scripture describes her response like this:

> The Samaritan woman said to him, *"You are a Jew and I am a Samaritan woman. How can you ask me for a drink?"* (For Jews do not associate with Samaritans) (John 4:9).

There was so much racism coursing back and forth between Jews and Samaritans that the very act of asking her a question validated her existence and significance in a way that shocked her. But the bottom line here is that Jesus asked a question, and then listened to her answer.

When you teach your selfie-focused teenagers to ask a question and truly listen to their peers, you are showing them how to pursue others with love.

"How Are You Really Doing?"

When I first met the woman who is now my wife, I was blown away. Yes, she was beautiful and all that jazz, but what really got my attention is that she paid attention. She cared about people.

Soon after we met she asked me, "How are you doing?" And like any self-assured male college student I responded, "Fine." Then she looked at me with her big blue eyes and said, "No, how are you *really* doing?"

I broke down and started sharing with her stuff that I really had been struggling with in my soul. To be honest, I've forgotten what I told her. I just remember telling her too much. Her simple act of love opened up a floodgate of struggles and emotions. More than her beautiful eyes, hair, face and features, it was her genuine love, expressed in a simple question that caught my heart.

My wife has been a public elementary school teacher for almost 20 years now. She teaches fifth grade, and pours out her love to her students, their parents and her fellow teachers. She asks questions and listens, and people flock to her like bees to pollen-filled flowers.

Even years later, her impact on her students has stood the test of time. For example, one of her former students who was then in college sent her a Facebook message. This student shared that she was a Biology major at a nearby university, and was really struggling with whether or not there was a God. Then this young lady confided that my wife was the only person she could remember who exemplified a Christianity that could be worth embracing, and she wanted to know more.

Soon after, the young lady put her faith in Jesus, and then immediately began to reach out to others with the good news. And it all started with a loving teacher who knew how to ask good questions, listen with her heart and not just with her ears, and point others toward Jesus.

In the same way, when you teach your teenagers to listen well, you equip them to love well.

 #GOSPELIZE *When you teach your teenagers to listen well, you equip them to love well.*

PERSUADE WITH TRUTH

> *Then Agrippa said to Paul, "Do you think that in such a short time you can persuade me to be a Christian?"*
>
> *Paul replied, "Short time or long—I pray to God that not only you but all who are listening to me today may become what I am, except for these chains"* (Acts 26:28-29).

The Greek word for "persuade" is *peitho*. According to *Thayer's Greek Lexicon*, it means "to make friends of, win one's favor, gain one's good-will...or to seek to win one."[4]

This meaning is far from the stereotype of a fast-talking used car salesman wheelin' and dealin' a person through the pearly gates. Instead, what the word connotes is winsomely seeking to win someone over. It reminds me of Paul's words to Timothy in 2 Timothy 2:24-26:

> *And the Lord's servant must not be quarrelsome but must be kind to everyone, able to teach, not resentful. Opponents must be gently instructed, in the hope that God will grant them repentance leading them to a knowledge of the truth, and that they will come to their senses and escape from the trap of the devil, who has taken them captive to do his will.*

This kind of gentle, yet persistent, persuasion is what draws the loudest of opponents in and takes them by the hand into the kingdom of God.

The Tower of Doom

Some years ago, my sweet Aunt Diane and my fun-loving cousins came out to Denver and headed to Six Flags with me. We were all ready for a day of fun in the mile high sun!

I enjoy a lot of things about amusement parks, but I'm not a big fan of rides that drop you at rapid rates of speed. Hence, the Tower of Doom was not on my list.

This is one of those rides that is pretty straightforward. It's a giant tower where you and your brave friends strap into seats that surround the base of it. Then it takes you slowly up, up, up into the air. Once you get to the top of the tower, you dramatically pause there taking in the view of the Rocky Mountains or the Denver skyline, depending on which way you are facing, before plunging at what feels like the speed of light toward the ground below. Midway through the ride, your stomach is in your mouth and sometimes the contents of your stomach are out of your mouth.

Not a fan.

So when my cousins said, "Tower of Doom! Let's go!" I said, "Tower of Doom? No!" Then they did something that never works with me, they started trying to shame me into going. They playfully taunted lines like, "You're a man, right?" "What? Are you a chicken?" "We're going to tell everyone that you were a big baby!"

With every mocking statement, my resolve stiffened. There was no way I would ever go on this ride from the abyss. That was until my Aunt Diane, who is a sweet-talking Southern belle, gently grabbed my hand and said with her Southern twang, "Y'all come with me."

Mesmerized by the verbal equivalent of sweet tea and porch swings, I said, "Okay," and began to follow her like a lamb to the slaughter. And before I figured out what was going on, I was in line for the Tower of Doom.

My cousins tried to coerce me, which totally didn't work! But my aunt gently persuaded me. I guess Grandma was right. You do catch more flies with honey than with vinegar.

In the same way, you can coach your teenagers on how to share the good news in a good way. You can equip them to persuade and not to coerce.

THE CAUSE CIRCLE

One of the tools we use at Dare 2 Share to help teenagers with the process of reaching their friends is THE Cause Circle. Students simply write down the names of three unreached friends in the circle, and begin to prayerfully and purposefully seek to reach them with gospel by praying for them with passion, pursuing them with love and persuading them with truth. And each new believer they lead to Christ can, in turn, begin to do the same thing with their *oikos*, as well.

This simple visual helps teenagers think through whom they want to reach out to with the good news of Jesus. Some youth leaders even incorporate a group-sized version of this circle on their youth

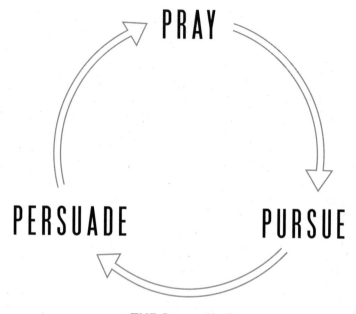

THE *Cause Circle*

Pray with passion. Pursue with love. Persuade with truth.

room wall, in an effort to consistently encourage their students to look at their circles of influence through the lens of relational evangelism.

TAKEOFF TO TOUCHDOWN

Speaking of dropping at rapid rates of speed from the sky to the ground, one day when I was down in Houston, my buddy, Vince, abruptly asked me, "Hey, wanna go flying? I have a new plane!"

"Um…sure," I responded. So we did.

It was a pretty sweet plane. But, as we were taxiing out to the runway, he began telling me that he was still getting certified in some area or other. He had his pilot's license, but still wasn't qualified to fly through clouds. What?!? (He hadn't yet passed his instrument rating test.) He also told me that his landings were still pretty rough.

At this point, I was wishing he would have told me all of this before we had gotten to the plane. But it was too late. I was committed. We took off, flew around Houston for awhile, and then landed... safely.

In the same way that Vince received training to fly a plane solo, you need to help your teenagers do the same when it comes to sharing their faith. Do your teenagers know how to share the gospel from takeoff to touchdown? Do they know how to bring the gospel up with their peers in a natural way—the takeoff? Can they explain the gospel clearly and completely—navigating the flight path? And do they know how to invite someone to put their faith in Jesus— landing the plane, so to speak?

At first they may not be totally competent and confident in dealing with turbulence (answering objections others may have with Christianity), but if they learn to takeoff, level off the plane at a comfortable altitude and land the plane, then that's a good start. You can help them get "certified" to fly through the clouds along the way.

One of the practical approaches we use at Dare 2 Share to help equip teenagers for give-and-take gospel conversations is called "Ask – Admire – Admit." This is shorthand for:

1. **ASK questions to understand where others are coming from spiritually.**
   "Can you tell me more about Wicca? I'm really not very familiar with it."

2. **ADMIRE what you can about what others believe.**
   "I really appreciate how Wiccans believe in a supernatural world."

3. **ADMIT that the reason you're a Christian is that you're so messed up that you need someone else to rescue you.** "May I share with you more about the One who rescued me from _____ (i.e., guilt, fear, hopelessness, pain or some other aspect of your personal faith story)?"

Whether or not you choose to use "Ask – Admire – Admit" or THE Cause Circle, get your students praying for their lost friends, and then coach them on how to nudge those friends gently, lovingly and consistently closer and closer to Jesus by pursing them with love and persuading them with truth.

FAITH SHARING RESOURCES

Dare 2 Share can help you train your teenagers to share the gospel from takeoff to touchdown. We have a free training app, the "Dare 2 Share" mobile app, which uses short videos to equip your teenagers for real world, give-and-take gospel conversations. You can also pick up a copy of the *Dare 2 Share Field Guide* from our online store at dare2share.org/store. This practical guide is basically a flight manual for teenagers and deals with everything from why to share, to what to share, to how to share your faith.

There's even a handy section in the back of the book to help your teenagers share their faith with 13 different worldviews—from atheists, to agnostics, to Mormons, to Muslims and more.

We also have a free engaging, interactive faith-sharing app called "Life in 6 Words" that will help your students clearly explain the gospel to others.

I encourage you to have your teenagers download the "Dare 2 Share" and "Life in 6 Words" apps and to pick up the *Dare 2 Share Field Guide*. These tools will help them learn how to share Jesus in a clear, compelling way and avoid a crash landing.

As you coach your students on how to engage their friends and acquaintances in deeper gospel conversations, you may also find Alan Hirsch's "m scale" of cultural barriers to the effective communication of the gospel helpful.[5] Check it out.

THEN THERE'S KEVIN

Although meaningful gospel conversations generally happen most effectively in the context of relationships, God can also use your teenagers to share the gospel with total strangers. Mission trips, service projects, VBS programs or going to the mall to do outreach are few examples of these kinds of opportunities. As a teenager, I would go to the Westminster Mall almost every week with a group of friends and engage other young people with the message of Jesus. I met Kevin at the Mall about 20 years ago. He was drunk, loud and kind of obnoxious. He and his buddies were mocking me for sharing Christ with them. He claimed to be some kind of thug from New York City. He shared stories of his time in the Big Apple and how he had taken a big bite out of it...and sold it at a pawn shop. Undaunted by his tough-guy façade, I asked him if he'd be willing to read a book when he sobered up. He agreed. I went out to my car and got a copy of *More than a Carpenter* by Josh McDowell, gave it to him and said goodbye.

Almost 10 years later, I got an email from a guy named Kevin. He was now a Sunday School teacher for teenagers at a local church. These teens had heard Kevin's testimony about meeting some crazy stranger at the Westminster Mall. They had also been to a Dare 2 Share Conference, where they'd heard my stories about sharing my faith at the Westminster Mall. They asked Kevin if the person who shared with him might be me. He thought maybe.

Kevin and I met soon after that. He threw the exact copy of *More than a Carpenter* that I had given to him years ago onto the table

GOSPEL ADVANCING STORIES FROM THE FRONT LINES
By Bill Freund

Despite all the apps, iPads and iPods and all the other electronic technology that we have, it will never change the fact that life is about relationships. Students want relationships. And they have relationships.

The average student has over 400 online and face-to-face friends. This provides a big opportunity for students to share Jesus. They all want their friends to come to know the Lord, but very few have a plan for doing that.

So we try to help them by giving them tools to be able to put together a plan to share with their friends. One of the ways we do that is by using the "Ask – Admire – Admit" approach to sharing your faith. We coach students to share with their friends by asking questions, admiring things about what they believe, asking more questions, admiring things, and then eventually taking that step of admitting that the reason they need Jesus is because they fall short, and they're not perfect.

In our youth ministry at Legacy, we give students an opportunity each week to have two "take homes"—one that drives them deep in their relationship with the Lord, and one that drives them wide in the relationship with their friends. For example, a deep take home is something that will cause our students to spend time with the Lord in prayer and in the Word each week. And then we also give them a take home that will help them share with their friends. Sometimes it's a video they can show their friend, sometimes it is a text, a question, or something that has to do with a relevant issue that's going on right now that will give them a topic they can turn toward a spiritual conversation.

in my office and said, "That was the book you gave me so many years ago." I opened it up and saw the notes he had written in the margins as he followed through on his promise to read it.

He explained to me that he carried 30 or 40 copies of *More than a Carpenter* in his car with him at all times to pass out to others. He especially loved reaching out to teenagers. And it all started as a result of me sharing Christ with a group of total strangers at a shopping mall.

Although this kind of experience is rare, who knows how many of those seeds planted by teenagers and adults sharing the gospel with strangers eventually bear fruit and multiply?

After all, the kingdom of God is expanded one gospel conversation at a time.

DO SOMETHING!

Getting your teenagers to engage their circles—and beyond— requires Spirit-empowered action. You must not just talk about it. You must do it. As the great preacher Charles Spurgeon told the young men he was training over 100 years ago:

> Brethren, do something; do something, do something! While societies and unions make constitutions, let us win souls. I pray you, be men of action all of you....Our one aim is to win souls; and this we are not to talk about, but do in the power of God![6]

What are *you* going to do about it?

SPICE IT UP...

Questions to help you and your leaders "Gospelize *YOUR* Youth Ministry."

1. Are you more comfortable sharing your faith with friends or strangers? Why?

2. After reading this chapter, what's your assessment of how our youth ministry program is doing at incorporating Value #2: "Relational evangelism drives it"?

3. Discuss the differences between being a quarterback and a coach when it comes to evangelism.

4. What did you think of the "Pray with Passion – Pursue with Love – Persuade with Truth" approach to relational evangelism?

5. Do you think THE Cause Circle would help our students be more purposefully about sharing their faith with their friends? Why or why not?

6. What three names would you put in your own personal Cause Circle?

7. Spend some time praying together for your unreached friends right now.

8. Discuss the "Ask – Admire – Admit" tool for initiating spiritual conversations.

9. Do you think the "Ask – Admire – Admit" approach would be helpful for our students?

10. Spend some time brainstorming specific ideas you might try that would help your ministry prioritize relational evangelism.

CHAPTER 06

FOLLOW THE LEADER

GOSPEL ADVANCING MINISTRY VALUE #3
Ministry leaders fully embrace and model it.

"What you see me doing with you, do with these teenagers."

This was the phrase that kept reverberating in our minds. There were about six of us youth ministry interns at this medium-sized Baptist church in Arvada, Colorado, and we were all excited about the new youth pastor. We huddled around his still clean desk as he explained his youth ministry philosophy to us.

He met with us weekly, so we met with our teenagers weekly.

He consistently prayed with us and for us, so we consistently prayed with and for our students.

He spent time outside the church with us, so we spent time outside the church with them.

Personal evangelism and relational discipleship were priorities with him, so personal evangelism and relational discipleship were priorities to us.

He led, and we followed. Then we led, and our students followed.

As a twenty-one-year-old youth ministry intern, I was witnessing Luke 6:40 fulfilled before my eyes: *"... everyone who is fully trained will be like their teacher."*

By the time this youth pastor moved on to his next ministry position, we had become like him in many ways. His example forever marked the way I view and do ministry, practically reinforcing Paul's words in 1 Corinthians 11:1: *"Be followers of me as I am of Christ."*

The disciples spent three and a half years following Jesus during His earthly ministry. And once they were indwelt with and empowered by the Holy Spirit at Pentecost, it was time for them to follow their leader down a new road—leading the church to glorify God and make and multiply disciples.

And guess what their leadership looked like? Jesus!

They were following the one and true leader, Jesus Christ. But Jesus was following the leader too. Jesus explained it this way in John 5:19: *"Very truly I tell you, the Son can do nothing by himself; he can do only what he sees his Father doing, because whatever the Father does the Son also does."*

Jesus followed the Father. The disciples followed Jesus. The Christian life is one big "game" of "follow the leader."

You remember the game "follow the leader" from your early elementary school years, right? All the kids line up behind one child who's been designated as "the leader." The leader does various motions and movements, and those behind him/her have to mimic.

Once Jesus ascended and sent His Holy Spirit to dwell within His disciples, they finally figured how to **really** follow the leader. Because the Holy Spirit now dwelt within them, He was the One leading them to follow the Lord Jesus Christ.

CHOOSING THE RIGHT KIND OF LEADERS

One of the measures of how successfully the disciples had mastered following their Master, was the degree of outrage their efforts elicited from the Sanhedrin. The Jewish leaders of the Sanhedrin were the same men who had conspired to have Jesus murdered. And now they saw the same dangerous DNA in His disciples—specifically Peter and John.

Like an angry principal, when the Sanhedrin caught wind of Peter and John preaching in the temple about Jesus' death, resurrection and offer of salvation to all who believe, they called them into "the office." When they confronted the two about their unrelenting Jesus-focused preaching, Peter and John answered: *"Salvation is found in no one else, for there is no other name under heaven given to mankind by which we must be saved"* (Acts 4:12).

Instead of cowering before a committee that could have them killed, these two men stood unflinchingly on the mission and message of Jesus. What was the Sanhedrin's response? Acts 4:13 describes it like this:

> *When they saw the courage of Peter and John and realized that they were unschooled, ordinary men, they were astonished and they took note that these men had been with Jesus.*

I especially love that last phrase: *"they took note that these men had been with Jesus."*

And what was Jesus like? He was defined by deep communion with the Father, powerful life-on-life investment in His disciples and a gritty gospel message that reached into the lives of the broken people He encountered!

That's what the Sanhedrin saw in Peter and John.

Is this what your teenagers see in you and the other student and adult leaders you have chosen to lead the way in your youth ministry?

How do you choose the right kind of leaders for your teenagers to follow? I'm talking here about your student leaders and adult volunteers. And I'm talking about you and your staff, because you and your leaders are the default thermostat for how much disciple-multiplying heat your entire youth ministry generates. If you and your leaders are cranked to high, then your students will tend to be the same. If you are lukewarm on evangelism, prayer and disciple multiplication, then your teenagers will tend to be lukewarm as well.

So what should you look for in student and adult leaders? What are the characteristics of a leader worth following? Don't let the description of Peter and John in Acts 4:13 paint over the many flaws both of these men struggled with, especially during the earthly ministry of Jesus.

John had some serious anger management problems. In Mark 3:17, Jesus gave John and his brother the nickname, "Sons of Thunder" after they asked God to destroy a Samaritan village with fire from heaven (Luke 9:54). That's the equivalent of a teenager asking God to strike an unbeliever with lightning for not accepting the gospel. John and his brother were ready to "go Old Testament" on anyone who seemed to be blocking the advancement of God's kingdom.

While John struggled with his temper, Peter struggled with his pride.

Jesus accurately predicted that the disciples would abandon Him when the situation got dangerous. But Peter bragged to Jesus: *"Even if all fall away on account of you, I never will"* (Matthew 26:33).

What an arrogant thing to say. And why did he say it? Because he was arrogant!

I know this Peter. I've been this Peter. Sometimes I still am this Peter…proud, boastful and determined to be the best, or at least better than the rest.

How did Jesus respond to Peter's braggadocious statement?

> "Truly I tell you," Jesus answered, "this very night, before the rooster crows, you will disown me three times."
>
> But Peter declared, "Even if I have to die with you, I will never disown you." And all the other disciples said the same (Matthew 26:34-35).

Peter's prideful boasting was infectious. All of Jesus' disciples began to brag about their unshakeable commitment to Him in the face of danger.

But when push came to shove, Peter shoved the soldiers out of the way and ran for his life with the rest of the disciples into the dark of night.

Peter failed. He failed miserably. And so did his fellow disciples. That fateful night that Jesus was arrested in the Garden of Gethsemane, the hearts of the fleeing, terrified, friend-abandoning disciples were dark with despair and defeat.

Three denials later, Peter heard the rooster crow, caught eye contact with Jesus and ran out weeping bitterly (Luke 22:61-62). His unshakeable resolve had been shaken. His self-dependence and flesh-fueled determination to follow Jesus unraveled behind him with every step he took.

But Jesus didn't give up on Peter because of his failure. Instead, Jesus approached Peter on the shore of the Sea of Galilee after His resurrection and before His ascension. Jesus cooked some bread and fish for him and a half dozen or so of His fellow disciples.

After the meal, Jesus had a talk with Peter that changed everything (John 21:15-19).

Peter had gotten the pride scraped from his soul, and now he was ready to lead, because for the first time, he would lead with humility and dependence on God, instead of with prideful self-dependence. He finally knew it wasn't about him or his ability to love Jesus. It was about trusting in Jesus to empower him, because, as Jesus reminded Peter and the disciples in John 15:5, *"Apart from me you can do nothing."*

THE TASTE OF DEFEAT

Like Peter and John, leaders worth following often know the taste of defeat.

My grandpa used to say, "That guy's a good guy. He just needs to get his @#%! kicked once."

Life knows how to kick it. And God uses those divinely sanctioned beatings to prepare us—and our best student and adult leaders—for powerful ministry.

Some of the best youth ministry leaders I have ever met have tasted defeat deeply, and are now learning to walk in victory humbly. There's something about loss and brokenness that can scrape the pride off of us, and prepare us to be used by God in the way He originally intended.

It could be a firing, a marriage struggle, a personal addiction, a financial disaster, a physical ailment or a failure to achieve a goal, but God often uses defeat or suffering to propel us forward in a new way that is defined by humility and dependence on Him.

As the great Apostle Paul ministered throughout the book of Acts in huge and powerful ways, there was a secret battle going on in the depths of his soul. He referred to his secret battle as his "thorn in the flesh," and pleaded for God to remove it on at least three different occasions. But God's answer was the same in every case: *"My grace is sufficient for you, for my power is made perfect in weakness"* (2 Corinthians 12:9a).

Eventually, Paul understood that the reason God allowed him to taste defeat in this particular area was to keep him humble and dependent on God. Upon realizing this Paul proclaimed to the believers at Corinth:

> *Therefore I will boast all the more gladly about my weaknesses, so that Christ's power may rest on me. That is why, for Christ's sake, I delight in weaknesses, in insults, in hardships, in persecutions, in difficulties. For when I am weak, then I am strong* (2 Corinthians 12:9b-10).

As A.W. Tozer once said, "It is doubtful whether God can bless a man greatly until He has hurt him deeply."[1]

Maybe this speaks to you personally as a youth leader. Your struggles and failures may feel like a giant weight on your back that is crushing you. But that weight can be a good thing, *if* it forces you to your knees. Because it's on our knees, in utter dependence on Jesus, that we can lead our teenagers in authenticity and with divine impact.

Now in Acts 4:13, a few months after his devastating denial of Jesus, we find Peter standing before the same Sanhedrin who condemned his King. But this time, not only did Peter refuse to deny Jesus; he refused to stop speaking His message. The difference between the old Peter and the new Peter is the distance between trusting in his own willpower and relying on his faith in the indwelling Holy Spirit.

It's Peter's post-Pentecost passionate pursuit of Jesus and authentic embodiment of gospel advancing values that made him such a powerhouse in the first eleven chapters of Acts. He was always a leader, but now he was a humble, trusting and authentic leader who the other disciples gladly followed.

In the same way, teenagers are longing for humble authenticity, especially in the adult leaders who pour into their lives. My youth ministry mentor who was the head of the Youth Ministry Department at Colorado Christian University used to tell us that teenagers are secretly asking three questions about the adult leaders who pour into their lives:

1. Do you love Jesus?
2. Do you love me?
3. Are you for real?

Look for leaders who can answer "Yes" to all three of those questions. Look for leaders whose lives are defined by humility, authenticity and dependence on God as they seek to live out gospel advancing values in their personal lives.

So standing before the Sanhedrin in Acts 4:13 stood two men who had learned what it meant to walk in this strangely divine mixture of humility and boldness. But this verse also shows us two defining characteristics of the leaders we should be and should be looking for to lead our teenagers.

ORDINARY PEOPLE, LIVING COURAGEOUSLY

"When they saw the courage of Peter and John and realized that they were unschooled, ordinary men, they were astonished..." (Acts 4:13a).

Leaders worth following are ordinary people, courageously living out gospel advancing values.

There was nothing outstanding about Peter, John or the rest of the disciples. They weren't highly educated. Most of them came from blue-collar backgrounds. And there's a good chance that most of them had been overlooked by other rabbis as potential disciples.

You see, in this culture every good Jewish boy wanted to follow a rabbi someday. It was the best thing that could happen to you as a young Jewish man. Between the ages of five and ten or so, you would go to Beth Sefer, a school associated with the local synagogue, where you would master the basics of the Torah. And when I say master, I mean memorize. You would also begin to learn the family trade. The best of the best of these students would move on to Beth Midrash. At this school, also taught by a rabbi, you would master the rest of the Old Testament Scriptures and begin to learn various interpretations of these passages and receive instruction on how to apply them to your own life. During this time, you would experience your first Passover in Jerusalem—like Jesus did in Luke 2:41-42.

By the age of 14 or so, the best of the best of these students would move on. You would intensely study for "the test," and would pursue the process of interviewing with a famous rabbi in the hope that you would be selected to travel about the countryside with him. After the interview, you would either be invited to "come, follow me," or be sent back home to work in the family business.[2]

Jesus' disciples were, most likely, all a part of Beth Sefer. A few may have made it on to Beth Midrash. But none were extraordinary enough to have been invited to follow an actual rabbi. Like most Jewish boys, they didn't measure up to the quality level desired and demanded by the religious system of the day. Instead, they'd turned full time to occupations that reflected their blue-collar roots.

So when Jesus invited Peter, Andrew, James and John in Matthew 4:18-21 to come and follow Him, it was a big, big deal. These working men had not been selected as disciples by a respected

Jewish rabbi of the time. But now Jesus, the very Messiah Himself, the King of kings, Lord of lords, Rabbi of rabbis, had said, *"Come, follow me."*

Sometimes we make the same mistake the respected rabbis of Jesus' day did when it comes to finding our disciples. We tend to look to the extraordinary, outstanding ones who can quote the verses. Those who are clean and shiny draw our interest. And sometimes these teenagers *are* the best ones to lead. But often, it's the grittier, scuffed and scarred teenagers—and adults—who have more potential to be true leaders.

You see, it's not always those who diligently set up the chairs in the youth room who are qualified to lead. It's the ones who can set up the chairs, *and* then fill them with the peers they are seeking to reach with the good news who are most qualified to lead! It's the high will/raw skill teenagers—those who are motivated, but often unequipped—who can be transformed with the right training into high will/high skill leaders.

Sadly, it's sometimes your teenagers who know the Bible best, who follow it the least. I'm sure you've encountered these kinds of students who can spout Scripture, but are lacking the heart and passion that comes from a personal, intimate, vibrant and growing relationship with Jesus. If teenagers are not actively living and sharing their faith, they all too easily become like sponges full of milk. If they don't wring out the milk of the Word to others through love, service and evangelism, they sour and spoil.

That's why I thank God that I attended a Christian school growing up that demanded that we wring ourselves out in evangelism. Sharing the gospel was central to everything we did and everything we talked about. It was even tied into math class! As a result, we were ready to lead.

The 10% Rule

Courageous leadership implies a mission and a destination. You and your leadership team are leading others toward that ultimate mission given to us by Jesus Himself in Matthew 28:19: *"Go and make disciples of all nations..."*

You need student and adult leaders who are willing to get in the trenches and lead the way—one prayer at a time, one gospel conversation at a time, one disciple at a time. And over time, it will turn the tide and get your group to what Malcolm Gladwell famously dubbed "the tipping point."[3]

Academic research backs up this principle that the few can lead the way and greatly impact the many:

> Scientists at Rensselaer Polytechnic Institute (RPI) have found that when just 10 percent of the population holds an unshakable belief, their belief will always be adopted by the majority of the society.[4]

Their study called these 10%ers "True Believers."

The key to any successful sociological movement is to have 10% of the population 100% committed to it. If you take a look at history, both recent and distant, you'll see that it wasn't the 90% that changed the culture around them. Instead, it was the fully committed 10% who changed everything. Consider these examples...

- How could a relatively small group of gay rights activists drive a tolerance agenda in America so loudly and proudly that in a few short decades homosexual marriage is now the law of the land?

- How could a marginalized group of political radicals in Germany rise from an obscure party to a dominating European force that not only commandeered and captivated Germany, but also ushered in World War 2 and the Holocaust?

- How could a small group of fanatical Muslims infiltrate and topple entire political systems?

- How could the combined preaching power of two extra-ordinary evangelistic extremists named George Whitefield and John Wesley inspire a movement that would turn America and England upside down with the gospel?

- How could a tiny handful of mostly Jewish believers take the gospel from Jerusalem to Rome in less than thirty years without Twitter, e-mail, www.theapostlejohn.com, cell phones, planes, trains or automobiles?

The answer to every one of these questions is through the leadership of "the fully committed 10%."

This statistic has amazingly powerful implications for the way we do ministry. As ministry leaders, we are typically taught to reach the masses at all costs. But this is counterintuitive to the way Jesus approached His ministry. Yes, He ministered to the masses. But He "radicalized" a small group of more fully committed followers who He nicknamed apostles, and after He ascended into heaven, they radicalized the rest. Isn't it interesting that of the one hundred and twenty in the upper room, there were twelve apostles? That's 10%.

Hmm….

I remember experiencing the power of this principle as a part time youth intern. Because I was also a full time roofer, I knew that the time I had to really invest in these teenagers was limited. So I decided to intentionally focus on the leaders. For the first several months, I consistently challenged the teenagers in my group to go all in for following Christ, and if they were willing to *truly* do that, to let me know.

Three out of the group eventually said "yes." So I poured my time into them. We spent time before and after youth group together. I invested in them. I took them out sharing their faith and got more deeply involved in their lives.

I was in charge of the seventh graders, and since there were less than 30 of them, with three fully committed twelve-year-olds in the group, we had more than enough critical mass to impact the climate of the entire group. Soon, I began to realize that these teenagers had become the leaders for the entire group. By God's grace, the pace I set for them soon began to set the pace for the youth group.

Teens Just Like Sarah

Sarah first put her faith in Christ at one of our Dare 2 Share conferences. Soon after that, she attended Lead THE Cause (LTC), a week-long leadership training D2S and Sonlife now partner together on. LTC is designed to turn ordinary teenagers—ones with high will—into extraordinary leaders.

I recently received a note from Sarah that, with her permission, I want to share with you.

> Dear Greg and really the whole D2S staff,
>
> For the past two years I have attended Lead THE Cause and have been given the opportunity to hear from God.
>
> My first year at LTC challenged me immensely. You see, I had just decided to give my life to Christ at the *Follow* conference in Chicago, and my heart was so excited for the new adventure I had just begun. LTC allowed me time to dream big for THE Cause, and equipped me with the knowledge and wisdom it took to lead 70-something peers to know Christ and make Christ known in a school Bible study. This study will be starting its third consecutive year this fall, still allowing kids to meet with fellow believers as they pray and plan to change their school; all because of how God equipped me through my week in Colorado at LTC.

But my biggest appreciation is for last year's LTC. My heart and life was changed once again. At the beginning of the camp, I was thrilled to hear how to reach my school and community for Jesus again, but I wasn't ready for what God had in mind. Right before you gave the sermon in the mountains, I asked you how you keep your passion for the lost. And you answered me with, "Feelings and passion will come and go, but it is all by faith. Faith in Christ comes first, and then God will give you passion." With that racing through my mind, you started your sermon on hell, eternity and passion for the lost. I was still oblivious at the time to God's plan, but my heart was so broken, and so ready to do something. At the end of your sermon, you looked me straight in the eyes and said, "Sarah, go and make disciples of all nations." And that has completely rocked me, and made me strive after what God's plan is for me.

I want to thank you for that, because through trust and faith in His cause, God is sending me.

This summer I will be spending the last week of June and the whole month of July in Nepal with a passionate team, as we make disciples in one of the most demonic parts of the world.

I send this letter to simply show you a small segment of the fruit this ministry is bearing. Thank you for all that you and the whole D2S staff do, because through this ministry I have found salvation, passion and finally the trust and willingness to make disciples of ALL nations.

I am sad I won't be able to attend LTC this summer, but you will always be in my prayers. So in closing, I am eternally grateful and excited to see what God will do this year through your ministry.

For THE Cause,

Sarah

After attending her first year of Lead THE Cause, Sarah decided to let go of playing her favorite sport for the year, hockey, so she could focus on reaching her school for Christ! (She's from Minnesota where giving up hockey is a big deal!) Talk about being a 10%er! She was willing to sacrifice something that was dear to her, so she could win at something that was even dearer, reaching her school with the good news!

Every week for an entire school year, she would meet with her fellow students, challenge them to live and share their faith and lead them in praying for their peers to come to Jesus.

That school year lives were changed, souls were saved and a school was rocked for Jesus.

Now Sarah has even bigger plans to advance God's kingdom, both at her school and around the world.

Sarah is an ordinary teenager, with an extraordinary passion to serve God. She is the kind of student leader youth leaders need to find and foster. And they are out there. They may not know it yet. You may not know it yet. But they are waiting to be inspired—just like Sarah. They are waiting to be equipped—just like Sarah. And they are waiting to be unleashed—just like Sarah!

The Way to the Brain

To find your 10%ers, give your teenagers a great big motivation to live and share their faith. Help them know why it is so important. Jesus did this by sharing real stories and raw truth. These real stories followed Jesus everywhere He went. The disciples saw these stories fleshed out in real life. They saw loose women converted and hedonistic tax collectors transformed before their very eyes.

Jesus also provided His followers with a motivation for sharing His message by speaking raw truth. He talked about God's dramatic love for us (remember the Prodigal Son?), but He also talked about the reality of hell. In fact, He talked about hell more than anyone else in the New Testament. He spoke of heaven, forgiveness, transformation and the purpose of life. Jesus relentlessly inspired His disciples with real stories and raw truth.

It has been said that the key to great preaching is great subjects. I encourage you to unpack these same kinds of great subjects—salvation, heaven, hell, the cross, Judgment Day and the return of Christ—for your teenagers. God can use these foundational spiritual realities to inspire your students to go all in and serve Him.

When people find out that I do teen evangelism training for a living, they inevitably ask, "Isn't it hard to train teenagers to share their faith?" And my answer is always the same, "No! After you motivate a teenager to share the gospel, training them is easy!"

We say it all the time at Dare 2 Share, "The way to the brain is through the rib cage." In other words, if you grab a teenager's heart, then their brain will follow.

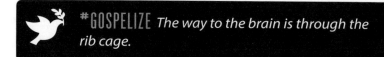

#GOSPELIZE *The way to the brain is through the rib cage.*

To find your future 10%ers pray, pray, pray, and then inspire, inspire and inspire some more! But before you do, remember that the 10% starts with you.

A young pastor once asked the great revivalist Gypsy Smith how he could start a revival at his church. The evangelist simply told him to go home, draw a circle on the floor with a piece of chalk and kneel within that circle. Smith then instructed the young man to pray for revival for everyone on the inside of that circle, and once he did that, he would start to see revival on the outside of the circle.

So get a piece of chalk, draw that circle and kneel within it. May you be the first to join the 10%. Then call your teenagers to do the same! It will often be the most unlikely of teenagers who join you in this quest—the ones that a rabbi would have overlooked 2,000 years ago. But they may very well be the kind of followers Jesus would have picked.

A GROWING RELATIONSHIP WITH JESUS

The final leadership insight that can be drawn from Peter and John's situation in Acts 4 is that leaders worth following relentlessly cultivate their relationship with Jesus.

While the disciples had been with Jesus over the previous three and a half years of His earthly ministry, the amazing new spiritual reality was that they were even closer to Jesus after Pentecost. As a result of the indwelling presence of His Holy Spirit, they were now constantly with Jesus on a day by day and moment by moment basis.

Peter and John had passionately pursued and relentlessly cultivated their walk with Jesus through prayer, fellowship, communion and the Word (Acts 2:42). They weren't surfing off the waves of a past relationship with Jesus when He walked the earth with them; they were surfing on a tsunami of their current relationship with Him every single day.

Are your student and adult leaders passionately and relentlessly cultivating their relationship with Jesus? Are their prayer lives strong? Do they spend time in the Scriptures on a consistent basis? Do they have relationships with brothers and sisters in Christ that go beyond the superficial? Are they seeking to live in a God-honoring way in every area of their lives? This doesn't mean that they never fail, but that that their lives are defined by failing forward in their quest to serve Jesus.

Without consistent attention to the secret areas of their lives, without a daily cultivation of their relationship with Jesus, they become a moral failure waiting to happen.

Joe's Story

I'll call him Joe, anyway. He was a rock star youth leader, one of the best I've ever seen. He was a guy I was beginning to invest in personally, because I thought that someday he might be able to step up and help me train teenagers and youth leaders nationally.

This guy had built a youth ministry with leaders who were 10%ers. This group made disciples who made disciples! I had personally met teenagers from Joe's group who'd been led to faith by other teenagers, who'd been led to faith by other teenagers—third generation teen-on-teen discipling.

His youth group was quickly becoming one that I pointed other youth leaders to as a model of what a gospelized youth ministry should look like. It wasn't perfect, but it was pretty close.

But somewhere along the line, Joe must have stopped cultivating his relationship with Jesus. Whether it was a slow erosion or a quick one, I don't know. But what I do know is that I got a shocking call from his wife one day.

He had fallen sexually with a girl from the youth group. It not only devastated his wife and children, it devastated his entire church and the churches that had been inspired by his example.

It devastated me, as well. It broke my heart for the girl involved. It broke my heart, because I felt for the teenagers in his youth group. It broke my heart, because the name of Jesus was being dragged through the mud as a result.

It also shook me, because I knew if it happened to Joe, it could happen to me. If I didn't keep my relationship with Jesus strong on a daily basis, I was a decision away from doom.

I tell this story not to point fingers. I tell it to bring urgency to your prayers for yourself, your adult leaders and student leaders (and me, for that matter). Each of us must relentlessly pursue Jesus moment by moment and actively cultivate an ever deepening relationship with Him.

FINDING THE RIGHT LEADERS

Leaders worth following have often tasted defeat, tend to be ordinary people who courageously live out gospel advancing values and relentlessly cultivate their relationship with Jesus. But how do you find them?

Here's my formula: identify, pray and stalk.

Identify exactly what it is you're looking for in a student leader and adult leader. What are the qualities that make the ideal kind of leader you would like to have in your youth ministry? Make sure the seven gospel advancing values are on that list. And remember that what they may lack in skill, they can make up for in will. Look for the ready and willing, and through the power of the Holy Spirit, you can make them able.

Pray that God would give you wisdom to know who to choose. In Luke 6:12b-13 it says:

> *...Jesus went out to a mountainside to pray, and spent the night praying to God. When morning came, he called his disciples to him and chose twelve of them, whom he also designated apostles.*

It surprises people oftentimes that Jesus had way more than 12 disciples. He took many disciples with Him—including many women according to Luke 8:1-3—and at one point He chose 72 disciples out of the crowd of other disciples to go on a special evangelistic campaign (Luke 9:1).

GOSPELIZE YOUR YOUTH MINISTRY

How did Jesus choose them? Prayer! Ask God to raise up leaders, and ask Him to help you identify those He has raised up!

By the way, this is why I advise youth leaders to NEVER do the all-call Sunday morning announcement that the youth ministry needs more leaders. If you recruit leaders this way, you will get the ones you prayed you would not get. So what do you do instead?

Stalk the best to be leaders in the youth ministry!

Find adults in your church who are modeling a gospel advancing lifestyle, and talk them into it! If that doesn't work, take them to Titus 2:1-6 where older men are challenged to pour into younger men, and older women are challenged to pour into younger women. If that doesn't work, then tell them that God told you to tell them to be a youth ministry volunteer leader. (Just kidding!)

But what you can do is give them a vision of where you are headed, explain why you think they are the best choice to lead teenagers and share stories of changed lives in your youth ministry. Like a dog with a bone, don't let it go until they tell you "no."…And maybe not even then.

GOSPEL ADVANCING STORIES FROM THE FRONT LINES
By Jim Barringer

I've had the privilege of serving in youth ministry full time for almost 20 years. I've learned a lot of lessons, and unfortunately, I've learned a lot of lessons the hard way. Hopefully, I can help prevent that for you. One of the lessons I've learned the hard way is that I can't do it by myself. Much as I try, much as I put in the hours, it really doesn't bear much fruit.

I remember when I was first starting out in youth ministry and the church I came to had three youth leaders. I was so excited to build a team, rally the troops, cast a vision and "go, go, go." I set up an appointment with each of these three leaders, so I could get to know them, hear their heart and understand why they were involved in the youth ministry. I wanted to see how I could help coach them and inspire them to fulfill God's call in their life.

At the end of the week, after meeting with each of them individually, instead of having three youth leaders, I had one. Two of them bailed on me. They said, "Hey man, we're so glad you're here finally. We're exhausted, and you're the professional. We're so glad that you can do this now."

I spent a lot of those first years trying to figure out how to build a team, inspire them and work toward my long-term goal, which is discipleship. And that's the ministry model I want to inspire you to build towards. Not just a giant youth ministry. Not just a ministry with great fantastic programs, great music and great teaching. All those things are great—they're legitimate. But what we're really called to do is to make disciples. And not just make disciples, but make disciples who make disciples. It was Howard Hendricks who said: "You can impress people from a distance, but you can impact them only up close."[5]

Do you want students who love God's Word? Then you need to find leaders who love God's Word. If you want students who are willing and able to share their faith with their lost friends, then you need to find leaders who are willing and able to share their faith with their lost friends.

Do a self-assessment first, before you begin recruiting and building a team, ask yourself whether you're living those values and working toward that vision. Is this something that you fully embrace and are living out with your life?

Then as you reach out and are trying to find people to build your team, be looking for people who agree and buy into those same kinds of values. As you describe your vision and what you're working towards, make sure it's crystal clear for them. Make sure they understand what it is that you're working towards.

I was just talking to a couple of our youth leaders the other day. They had a gal in their small group who was really struggling. So what did they do? They camped out in front of her house, because they couldn't get a hold of her. She wasn't responding to their text, she wouldn't answer their phone calls. She wouldn't respond to their emails. So they went to her. They literally lived out the one lost sheep principle. They left the 99 and they went to this girl. They pursued her.

Another group of leaders had a gal in their group who was really struggling, and because of things going on in her life, she had distanced herself from the rest of the group. But they knew that this gal had a job serving as a waitress, so they rallied the other students in their group and they went to see her where she was serving as a waitress. And they just made it happen for her. They tipped her well, encouraged her and rallied around her.

That's the kind of model of ministry that we've strived and struggled to build over a long period of time. Jesus says in Luke 6:40: *"The student is not above the teacher, but everyone who is fully trained will be like their teacher."* We can't do that far away. And you can't do that by yourself.

I didn't ask those leaders to go do those things. I didn't ask them to camp in front of that girl's house. I didn't ask them to go to that restaurant. They just knew that those were the right things to do. They knew it because God has called them to that group of students, and they knew it because they understand the principle of the one lost sheep. They understand that relationships aren't built through a medium like text messaging. It's got to be life-on-life. And that's the kind of a ministry where the leaders fully embrace the vision and live it out with their lives. That is discipleship. That is life-on-life.

Sometimes our best potential student leaders are also very busy with other things—like sports, hobbies, academics and so on. Make a case with them that the very best way they can use their gifts is to advance the kingdom of God. Take what you can get of their time, and make the most of it. Whatever they are involved with, if it involves other people, it can be used to impact your youth ministry *if* you teach them how to make disciples along the way.

I was once at a donor meeting with a small group of adults in Columbus, Ohio. As I was talking about youth groups advancing THE Cause of Christ across the Buckeye State, one of our donors, Greg, choked up. He interrupted and said, "My kids are too involved in their school activities to really make a difference for God. My son is on the football and baseball teams. My daughter is a cheerleader and is involved with other school things. They don't have time to go and make disciples!"

I shared with Greg that when Jesus said, *"Go and make disciples"* it can literally be translated, *"As you are going, make disciples,"* because the word "go" in the Greek is a participle, it can be translated "as you go" instead of just plain "go." It's a descriptive, not a directive. The directive is to "make disciples" the descriptive is "as you go…" That means that as your teenagers are going to practice, they can make disciples. As they are involved with football, baseball, cheerleading or whatever, they can make disciples. As a matter of fact, if all they are involved with is youth group, it's going to be hard for them to actually make disciples.

Some of your best student leaders may be your busiest student leaders. But in their busyness, as they are going, they can be taking care of business when it comes to making and multiplying disciples.

May God multiply this type of leader to help you lead your youth ministry!

SPICE IT UP...

Questions to help you and your leaders "Gospelize *YOUR* Youth Ministry."

1. In what ways is the Christian life like a game of "follow the leader"?

2. Do you agree that leaders worth following know the taste of defeat? Why or why not?

3. Discuss the following statement: "Teenagers are secretly asking three questions about the adult leaders who pour into their lives: Do you love Jesus? Do you love me? Are you for real?" Are the answers to those questions obvious to the students in your group? What other questions may they be asking about their adult leaders?

4. Are you currently courageously living out gospel advancing values?

5. Would you characterize yourself as a 10%er when it comes to advancing the gospel?

6. Brainstorm together which students in your group might fall into the "high will/raw skill" group (those defined as 10%ers)?

7. What could you do to help them become more equipped to make disciples who make disciples?

8. How are you doing at passionately pursuing and relentlessly cultivating your walk with Jesus through prayer, fellowship, communion and the Word? Would it help to have a personal accountability partner? Why or why not?

9. Based on the formula "identify, pray and stalk," are there any adults in our church we should be inviting to join our youth ministry team?

10. Take an honest assessment. How are your adult and student leaders doing at life-on-life discipleship with your students?

CHAPTER 07

GO EXPONENTIAL

GOSPEL ^ADVANCING MINISTRY VALUE #4
A disciple multiplication strategy guides it.

Can you feel the excitement and forward propulsion of the gospel pulsing through the book of Acts as you read the following verses?

*"Those who accepted his message were baptized, and about **three thousand were added to their number that day"** (Acts 2:41).*

*"And the Lord **added to their number daily** those who were being saved"* (Acts 2:47).

*"But many who heard the message believed, and **the number of men grew to about five thousand"** (Acts 4:4).*

*"Nevertheless, **more and more men and women believed** in the Lord and were added to their number"* (Acts 5:14).

*"So the word of God spread. The number of disciples in Jerusalem **increased rapidly,** and **a large number** of priests became obedient to the faith"* (Acts 6:7).

*"But the word of God **continued to increase and spread"*** (Acts 12:24).

*"The word of the Lord **spread through the whole region"*** (Acts 13:49).

*"So the churches were strengthened in the faith and **grew daily in numbers"*** (Acts 16:4).

*"...the word of the Lord **spread widely and grew in power"*** (Acts 19:20).

Down deep inside you know you want it. You long for your youth group to grow in all the right ways—spiritually of course, but also with a ton of new believers. Because growing with new disciples who are being made and multiplied is a key marker that you're making a difference, not just in the lives of the teenagers inside your youth room walls, but in the lives of those outside of your Christian bubble.

And there's something dangerously exciting when these teenagers begin to come to small group and youth group. New believers often don't have a "religiously correct" grid, so they can easily drop an f-bomb after worship, "This God stuff is %$&#@! awesome!" They can be talking about sharing Christ with their friends in the parking lot after youth group while smoking a joint—especially in my home state of Colorado—without thinking twice. New believers often don't know any better.

But it's this same raw excitement and gritty authenticity that can motivate them to reach their friends with the message of Jesus.

And soon disciples begin to multiply, and the same Acts-like adrenalin rush can begin to fill your youth group.

Yes, it's messy. So buy a mop, because it's worth the mess. It's worth every late-night conversation, awkward text and angry parent—probably one of the "fortress mentality" parents who don't want their teenagers around "those" kinds of kids.

But it's "those" kinds of kids—and adults—that the early church was filled with and fueled by. It was fishermen who reeked of fresh fish, prostitutes who reeked of cheap perfume and lepers who reeked of rotted flesh who flocked to Jesus in droves. These were the ones who knew they needed a doctor, and the church became their hospital, their hostel and their hope.

Admit it. When you read the book of Acts, you are secretly asking yourself, "Why not me? Why not here? Why not now?" If you're not asking those questions of yourself, you should be. Because you have the same mission as the disciples, and the same Holy Spirit living inside you, so there is no reason you can't have the same results!

The question is whether or not you are willing to put the same focus and effort into making and multiplying disciples as they were. If you're willing to do that, you will see your youth group grow in ways you never imagined, both spiritually and numerically! You will go exponential!

This is what we see happening progressively throughout the book of Acts.

PAUL'S EVOLVING GOSPEL ADVANCING STRATEGY

Paul was masterful at choosing strategic cities to spread the gospel to, and Thessalonica is a prime example of this. But he was only there for what appears to be less than a month. In Acts 17:1-3,

Luke writes:

> When Paul and his companions had passed through
> Amphipolis and Apollonia, they came to Thessalonica, where
> there was a Jewish synagogue. As was his custom, Paul went
> into the synagogue, and on three Sabbath days he reasoned
> with them from the Scriptures, explaining and proving that the
> Messiah had to suffer and rise from the dead. "This Jesus I am
> proclaiming to you is the Messiah," he said."

But then the Jewish leaders got upset, so Paul had to leave town
after only three Sabbath days. If I'm reading that right, he left town
somewhere between 21 and 27 days (I'm not all that good at math,
but I do know that four Sabbaths would be 28 days.) And what
was his time like during that brief, less-than-a-month stint? Paul
describes it in 1 Thessalonians 2:7-12 this way:

> Just as a nursing mother cares for her children, so we cared for
> you. Because we loved you so much, we were delighted to share
> with you not only the gospel of God but our lives as well. Surely
> you remember, brothers and sisters, our toil and hardship; we
> worked night and day in order not to be a burden to anyone
> while we preached the gospel of God to you. You are witnesses,
> and so is God, of how holy, righteous and blameless we were
> among you who believed. For you know that we dealt with each
> of you as a father deals with his own children, encouraging,
> comforting and urging you to live lives worthy of God, who calls
> you into his kingdom and glory.

Paul and his crew poured their lives into the Thessalonian new
believers, all while working secular jobs to fund their efforts.
This life-on-life investment into these newly minted Christians
propelled them forward in sharing their faith in no time! Just look
at how 1 Thessalonians 1:8 trumpets their spread of the gospel:
"The Lord's message rang out from you not only in Macedonia and
Achaia —your faith in God has become known everywhere."

The Greek word for "rang out" is *excheo*, which literally means "to echo out" or "reverberate." In their culture, this word was used to describe the sound of a trumpet blasting or thunder rolling. It is a big word that captures how effectively the Thessalonians were echoing out the message of the gospel all across Macedonia and Achaia—which constituted a sizable chunk of Greece.

In his commentary on this passage, J. Hampton Keathley explores the nature of *excheo*, explaining that it means "to cause to resound, sound or ring forth." Here's how he describes it:

> It seems that the Apostle saw the Thessalonians as amplifiers who first received the gospel message but then sent it reverberating on its way with increased power and scope much like an echo in the mountains... Apparently it was not through an organized evangelistic campaign that their witness went forth, though Paul's preaching in Thessalonica and elsewhere illustrates this approach. But it was through the personal lives and testimonies of these transformed individuals that neighbors heard about their faith in God. As they went the gospel was heard everywhere.[1]

This huge area was impacted by the gospel because Paul, literally over a matter of days, mobilized them to make and multiply disciples. And did they ever! In less than a month, Paul made enough of a relational investment in the Thessalonians that the good news of Jesus echoed all across their region.

What does all of this have to do with you and your teenagers?

When you bring a gospel advancing focus to your relational investment in your students, God can produce dramatic kingdom impact. Even while working another part time job—or a full time job like Paul—you can witness changed lives that change lives.

By the time Paul went on his third missionary journey, he was well aware of the reverberating impact of the gospel through the disciple-multiplying Thessalonians. My guess is that he began to think, "If this is what happened after a less-than-a-month investment, what would happen if I camped out for awhile and got serious about training the Ephesian believers to multiply?"

I am convinced—although I cannot categorically prove it scripturally—that Paul's strategy evolved from primarily doing outreaches at the synagogue, like he did during his first two missionary journeys, to primarily equipping believers to multiply disciples. And I believe it was the example of the Thessalonians' commitment to spread the good news across their region on their own, that helped convince him to make the switch. Let's take a look at how Paul's strategy changed in Ephesus.

THE SCHOOL OF TYRANNUS

By the time we get to Acts 19, we see Paul settling in at the School of Tyrannus in Ephesus for two whole years. This is the longest the biblical record indicates that he stayed anywhere on his missionary journeys. So why did he stay so long in Ephesus? Acts 19:8-10 gives us some clues. And these same clues will help you learn how to "go exponential" when it comes to making and multiplying young disciples in your group. Luke describes what happened like this:

> Paul entered the synagogue and spoke boldly there for three months, arguing persuasively about the kingdom of God. But some of them became obstinate; they refused to believe and publicly maligned the Way. So Paul left them. He took the disciples with him and had discussions daily in the lecture hall of Tyrannus. This went on for two years, so that all the Jews and Greeks who lived in the province of Asia heard the word of the Lord.

Take a look at that last phrase, "...so that all the Jews and Greeks who lived in the province of Asia heard the word of the Lord."

Let that sink in.

Everyone in the entire region of the province of Asia (modern Turkey) heard the good news.[2] That means every single person in every city, town and village within its boundaries heard the gospel through the efforts of this Gospel Advancing Ministry. That's like saying, "Everyone in the state of California heard the gospel through our youth group's efforts!"

How is that even possible? I guarantee you all the Jews and Greeks in the province of Asia didn't crowd into the synagogue to hear Paul preach! In the same way, not every teenager in your state will come to your outreach meeting. No, Paul had discovered a better way. Paul had developed a powerful strategy for disciple multiplication.

This strategy began with Paul reaching the Ephesians with the good news of Jesus every Sabbath in the synagogue (Acts 19:8). There Jews, as well as "God-fearing Gentiles" who had converted to Judaism, met every week for a Torah study. Because Paul had the background of being a Pharisee, he was a welcome guest preacher. Once he had the floor, he used his time as a way to point them to Jesus as the fulfillment of hundreds of Old Testament prophecies.

Many people came to Christ in the various synagogues when Paul preached the gospel. Others however, would question and argue, and sometimes even physically attack him (2 Corinthians 11:25). In these cities where Paul preached, he would help the believers form a church where they could grow spiritually, and could become the centerpiece ministry to reach others in their community with the good news of Jesus.

Paul did the same thing in Ephesus that he had done almost everywhere else. He used the synagogue as an outreach meeting. He preached there every Sabbath and tried to convince and convert as many as possible to faith in Jesus. He relentlessly pointed people to Jesus, and preached the good news of the gospel in every weekly meeting.

Before we go on to unpack what he did differently in Ephesus, and how it can help you go exponential in your own youth ministries, it's probably a good time to pause and ask how you are doing when it comes to giving the gospel message to your teenagers in the context of your own youth group on a weekly basis?

Are you consistently sharing the good news with your teenagers? Do they know that any time they bring an unreached friend to youth group that the gospel will be clearly presented?

I recall one youth leader who made a commitment to routinely give the gospel at some point during every youth group meeting. He did so consistently. But one night the program was running long, and he skipped it. And soon he got a text afterward, chewing him out for failing to share the gospel.

It was from a girl in his group who had been repeatedly inviting her friend to come out to youth group to hear the gospel. And it was that particular night her friend finally said, "Yes, I'll come with you." But it was that same night that this youth leader failed to share the message of Jesus.

He told me he would never skip it again.

But like I talked about in chapter 5, it shouldn't just be "on" that youth leader to give the gospel every week in his youth group meeting. It is also "on" that girl to share Jesus within her own circle of friends. Which brings us to the second part of Paul's "go exponential" strategy: Paul equipped the believers how to grow AND go—how to grow spiritually, and how to go evangelistically!

Let's take a closer look at verse 9 of this passage:

> *But some of them became obstinate; they refused to believe and publicly maligned the Way. So Paul left them. He took the*

*disciples with him and had discussions daily in the lecture hall
of Tyrannus.*

After three months of evangelistic meetings, Paul, as well as
those who had put their faith in Jesus as a result of his preaching,
moved to a local community college, the School of Tyrannus.
This school was probably used by the educational establishment
of the day in the early morning hours and later in the afternoon,
but was available for others to use/rent during the hot part of the
day (11 a.m.–4 p.m.).[3] It was most likely during this time Paul had
"discussions," and unpacked these disciples' newfound faith in a
deeper way, teaching them to grow deep in their relationship with
Jesus, while going wide with the good news.

Think about how pumped up the attendees at T-Ran U must have
been! If just *reading* the book of Ephesians gets you pumped up,
what about having the dude who wrote it as your professor—for
two years!

I'm sure they got so excited that they began to saturate their
circles—their *oikos*—with the gospel! They couldn't contain
themselves! This message was so compelling, and its impact on
their own lives so personally transforming, they had to tell friends,
neighbors, coworkers, family and strangers about the hope only
Jesus could offer.

Paul's Spirit-infused strategy dramatically culminated with
disciples being made and multiplied. The movement that erupted
from this School of Tyrannus spread from Ephesus to the outer
borders of the entire province. Within these borders, the seven
churches mentioned in the book of Revelation were fanned into
flame. And it was the students at the School of Tyrannus that had,
in the power of the Spirit, ignited the first sparks.

Imagine how it may have gone. Claudius, the newly converted
God-fearing Gentile, shared the gospel with his cousins from

Pergamum, who just happened to be in Ephesus that weekend for a little R and R. Instead of vacationing on the shores of the Mediterranean, they decided to hang out at T-Ran U for a few days and hear more about this message. After three days, they took it back to their family, friends and neighbors. Various versions of this scenario must have played out countless times over the next twenty-four months, until this province hit the gospel saturation point.

Not only was the entire region saturated with the good news, but the Ephesian believers were transformed by the very process itself. Although Revelation 2 was most likely penned a generation after Paul visited Ephesus, the following passage gives us a glimpse into what was happening among the Ephesian believers in those early years.

> *"To the angel of the church in Ephesus write:*
>
> *…I know your deeds, your hard work and your perseverance. I know that you cannot tolerate wicked people, that you have tested those who claim to be apostles but are not, and have found them false. You have persevered and have endured hardships for my name, and have not grown weary.*
>
> *Yet I hold this against you: You have forsaken the love you had at first."* (Revelation 2:1a, 2-4).

At one point, the Ephesians' love for God burned hot, and their hard work for God erupted out of their deep affection for Jesus like lava from Vesuvius. But somewhere along the line, that hot lava cooled to cold black rock. In Revelation 2, John is taking dictation from Jesus, warning them to fan that distant ember back into a white-hot flame again.

Could it be that the Ephesians were at their hottest when their gospel advancing flames were at their brightest? Could it be that the passionate, missional church they initially were had deteriorated into a stagnant, institutionalized poser—a program-driven shell of its former self?

It all boils down to this: when Jesus is your first love, you can't help but talk about Him. If you fall in love with evangelism, you'll eventually fizzle out. But if you fall in love—and stay in love—with Jesus, you'll always evangelize! Maybe that's why the first graduating class of the School of Tyrannus couldn't keep their mouths shut about Him.

I'm sure they studied the Old Testament harder, prayed longer and worshipped louder because they were watching Jesus multiply His kingdom through them.

 #GOSPELIZE *If you fall in love with evangelism, you'll eventually fizzle out. But if you fall in love with Jesus, you'll always evangelize!*

This same brand of gospel transformation can happen in your teenagers and throughout your community. You just need to get your students to fall passionately in love with Jesus, and equip them to tell everyone else about Him. That's when things go exponential!

The result for the province of Asia was a complete saturation of a region, with everyone hearing the good news and churches being planted by dudes like Epaphras who took the gospel to Colossae, Laodicea and Hierapolis (Colossians 4:12-13). How did Epaphras learn how to be a disciple multiplier? He learned it all from Paul—I'm guessing at the School of Tyrannus.

GOSPEL ADVANCING STORIES FROM THE FRONT LINES
By Julie Ritema

I'm a middle school youth pastor out in Sacramento, California, at Bayside Church. I'm super-excited to share with you about what it means to multiply your ministry by making disciples who make disciples. One of the coolest things I've seen in youth ministry is watching kids get excited about Jesus, because that's what it's all about! This past year one of our guys, Andrew, got so excited about Jesus that he shared the gospel with his friend, Haven. And then Haven went out and shared with his friend, James. How cool is that to watch?!? As kids get excited about Jesus, about having a relationship with Him, about the true gospel and about God's Word, they want to share with their friends!

I want to encourage you as a youth worker to get excited about Jesus yourself! Make sure that your programs are about Him and nothing else! I know the pressures that you have. You have to fill those seats and have great curriculum, awesome programs, exciting events, fun games and funny videos. I get that. But it starts with you. As a youth worker, you've got to make sure that you are discipling and equipping your students by mentoring them and showing them who Jesus is. When your walk with Jesus is thriving, it energizes the impact of your discipleship efforts with your students, as well.

And I also want to encourage you to go after your volunteer leaders and disciple them and mentor them, as well, because they play a huge part in the impact of your youth ministry.

When you make your youth ministry about Jesus it multiples. So stay with it. Don't give up. We all know the ups and downs of youth ministry, but trust God. Be encouraged that when you keep your ministry focused on Jesus, it's going to multiply and disciples are going to be made and multiplied.

WHAT'S YOUR DISCIPLE MULTIPLICATION STRATEGY?

Do you have an intentional strategy to "go exponential" with disciples who are being made and multiplied? What if you, like Paul, switched your strategy too? What if you moved beyond primarily using a "synagogue strategy" (bring your friends to youth group so I can share the gospel with them) to a "School of Tyrannus strategy" (I'll equip you to make disciples who make disciples)?

The strongest strategy I've ever come across for going exponential is Dr. Dann Spader's *4 Chair Discipling*. I highly recommend this strategy because it's based on the life and ministry of Jesus, and you can't go wrong with that! Jesus is the best model for believers to embrace and follow, not just because he is fully God, but because he is fully man! He lived as a man in full dependence on the Holy Spirit and showed us how to do the same. His example of Spirit-empowered disciple multiplication can be followed by us, because we have the same Holy Spirit inside us (Ephesians 1:13-14). Maybe that's why He guaranteed us in John 14:12:

> *"Very truly I tell you, whoever believes in me will do the works I have been doing, and they will do even greater things than these, because I am going to the Father."*

Empowered by the Spirit and following the example of Jesus, you can help your teenagers through the four chairs Spader explains in his book. You can help nudge them from Chair 1: Unbeliever; to Chair 2: Believer; to Chair 3: Worker; to Chair 4: Disciple Maker.[4] To learn more about this biblically robust and culturally relevant strategy, go to 4chairdiscipling.com. It will help you launch a "School of Tyrannus" in the context of your youth ministry and enable you to "go exponential" in ways you never imagined. Then you'll see disciple making at its best.

It's time to break out of the stereotypical model of discipleship that stalls out with two believers who've been saved for years sitting around once a week, going through a discipleship curriculum reminding themselves of stuff they should already know and already be doing.

Discipling is a verb—a life-on-life explosion of new life resulting in more lives being touched and transformed!

"PICK A NOTEBOOK!"

A few years back, my son and I traveled to Colombia on a trip with Compassion International to visit our sponsored child, Karla. It was one of those trips that mark you for a lifetime.

Thousands of churches in various countries around the world work with Compassion to build what they call a "project." These projects are a kind of base camp where they educate children, provide medical help, mentor and nurture their spiritual development. As the children move into their teenage years, they learn skills that help them in a trade. As I toured some of these projects with my son, I was more and more impressed with their efforts and with the pastors and leaders who ran them.

But looming in the back of my mind was the fear that the spiritual formation of these children was being back-burnered. After all, in some of the projects, there were over two hundred children and that seemed pretty overwhelming for a relatively small staff to handle when it came to spiritual development. So I decided to conduct my own little investigation.

I broke from the tour to talk to one pastor of one project who spoke fluent English. I asked him, "Pastor, I'm very impressed with what I see at your project, but how do you track where all these two hundred children are at spiritually?"

He paused for a moment and looked kind of perturbed that I would dare ask such a question. I soon found out why he was perturbed.

"Pick a notebook!" he said in a strong voice and smooth-as-silk Colombian accent.

"What?" I asked, not quite knowing what he was talking about.

"Pick a notebook!" he said again, this time pointing to the large bookshelf full of black binders behind me.

I picked one out and began to flip through it. The notebook represented one child currently active in that particular project, and it meticulously recorded how that child was doing in various areas. It had health records, school grades and family information. It also recorded when that child had indicated faith in Jesus as their Savior, the date of their baptism and how they were progressing in their faith.

When I put it back in its place, the pastor said with a smile, "Pick another notebook." It provided the same set of information about a different child.

When I scanned the large bookshelf, I saw two hundred black binders representing two hundred children, all of them tracking their students' growth on every level...including spiritually. I couldn't help but think to myself, "What if youth leaders were as meticulous in tracking the spiritual development of the teenagers in their youth groups as this small staff is with these two hundred children?

Of course there are multitudes of ways to accomplish this sort of tracking in a youth group context. But here's one approach I would encourage you to consider if you decide to use the "4 Chair Discipling" approach for making and multiplying disciples. Create a spreadsheet with the following five columns:

- **Column 1:** List the names of every teenager attending your youth group.

- **Column 2:** Do your best to assess what chair you think that teenager is currently sitting in:
  - Chair 1: Lost
  - Chair 2: Believer
  - Chair 3: Worker
  - Chair 4: Disciple Maker
- **Column 3:** Identify the action step that needs to be taken to nudge them toward the next chair.
- **Column 4:** Identify the student/adult leader assigned to give that teenager the nudge.
- **Column 5:** Identify the date that the action step is actually taken.

Once that action step has been accomplished, insert a new row in your spreadsheet for this student and build out the next new action step and timeframe.

Here's an example of what it could look like...

Name	"Chair"	Action Step toward Next "Chair"	Leader Assigned	Date Accomplished
John Smith	Believer	Recruit to help with greeting on Wed. nights	Matt	
Sarah Green	Worker	Establish ongoing weekly discipling schedule	Debb	
Emma Bond	Believer	Personally invite to next service project	Jenn	
Sam Banks	Lost	Invite to lunch with friend for gospel conversation	Jared	

RETURNING TO THE RANCH

This type of School of Tyrannus is what my own youth group, Christian Youth Ranch, was for me when I was a teenager. Yes, our pastor, Yankee, personally advanced the gospel, but more than that, he equipped us teenagers to share our faith. He entrusted us with the mission and the message of Jesus Christ. As a result, we saturated Arvada—and beyond—with gospel conversations.

Most of the teenagers who attended our group were not strangers we led to Jesus on the streets, but the friends, classmates, teammates and family members we engaged with the message of Jesus personally.

On Thursday nights, we had our main youth group meeting where we could bring our lost friends and acquaintances to hear the good news. But the expectation was that we would bring Jesus up in spiritual conversations with our friends before we even got to the meeting. And we were tasked with following up with them personally after the meeting, with what I've come to nickname "The Reverse Altar Call." Yankee never called teenagers forward to receive Christ. Instead, he equipped us to have conversations with our friends on the way out of the youth group meeting, or while we were driving back home with them. He coached us to ask simple questions. "Did what my youth leader say during the meeting make sense?" "Is there anything holding you back from putting your trust in Jesus right now?" This approach was so effective that I quickly lost track of the number of teenagers I was able to lead to Jesus after a Youth Ranch meeting. Then when we led someone to Jesus, we were also expected to disciple them.

Still, the main youth group meeting was only one part of this Gospel Advancing Ministry's efforts. The Thursday night Youth Ranch large group gathering—and I mean large, as in 800 teenagers— was a mere rallying point for a week of gospel conversations with our peers. There were also Sunday night leadership meetings that trained us on how to grow in the person of Christ and equipped us to share the message of Christ. During these meetings, we would share stories about our personal efforts to engage others in the gospel conversations. We would pray for each other's faith sharing opportunities and for our student-led discipleship training for new believers. We were passionate and purposeful about helping new believers get motivated and mobilized to share their faith, too, and make disciples who make disciples. Being part of the student leadership team meant we were responsible for driving the process of BOTH evangelism and discipleship.

As a side note, in the words of the late Mike Yaconelli, the typical youth ministry "has less seniors than juniors, and less juniors than sophomores." I'm fully convinced that one of the reasons for this is because we are not giving them a compelling reason to stay involved. The older teenagers get, the busier they get, and they have to weigh their priorities carefully. After all, they have ACTs to prep for, band to practice for, bosses to work for and sports teams to play for. We have to give them a bigger mission than all of those combined. We have to give them a reason to stay involved with youth group that outweighs all of these other competing interests. So when we build a Gospel Advancing, disciple-multiplying ministry that regularly sees lives changed and souls saved, we are giving them a bigger reason to stay involved.

Dodgeball, pizza and a Bible lesson may keep teenagers in youth group through the middle school years. But the older teenagers— and younger ones, as well—will be more compelled to stay, lead and thrive in a youth ministry that is making disciples, than in one that is just making s'mores (although they are truly delicious!).

Christian Youth Ranch kept many teenagers involved from middle school to high school graduation because it functioned as a School of Tyrannus in the lives of hundreds of teenagers. It had both practical, lifelong impact for those of us who were trained and equipped, and also eternal impact for those who heard the gospel and trusted in Jesus.

A MISSED THIRD GREAT AWAKENING

The Youth Ranch ministry movement which originally sprang out of South Florida fanned out across the nation, saturated my city and transformed my family with the good news of Jesus. In a North American context that "chatters" a lot about disciple multiplication, but rarely actually does it, I saw it in 3-D growing up. We had hundreds upon hundreds of disciples who had been made and multiplied by teenagers reaching other teenagers who had been reached by other teenagers.

I am convinced that it could have been the beginnings of The Third Great Awakening. And I don't say that lightly, because I'm a student of Great Awakenings. I truly believe the Youth Ranch movement was on the trajectory of being at least a national movement, if not an international one. But it came to a screeching halt when its founder and leader, Ray Stanford, fell into sexual sin and Florida Bible College stopped producing the large numbers of Youth Ranch leaders needed to continue to spread and lead the gospel advancing movement locally, nationally and globally.

It broke my heart.

I'm convinced that the reason that it all came apart is because this entire movement of disciple multiplication was often fueled out of planning, instead of prayer. Intercessory prayer was the caboose and not the engine, so this disciple multiplication train eventually came off the tracks.

But if thousands of teenagers were reached in my city, and tens of thousands (if not hundreds of thousands) of teenagers were reached across the United States, how many millions would have been reached if this movement was fueled by the Holy Spirit and prayer, instead of just good strategy and execution.

It's time.

It's time for an even stronger gospel advancing disciple multiplication strategy to begin…with you. What happened in the book of Acts can happen again. What I experienced as a teenager at Youth Ranch can be done even better in the power of the Spirit.

But you have to be willing to do what it takes to go exponential. Jesus showed us how. Paul showed us how. And now the Holy Spirit will show you how.

SPICE IT UP...

Questions to help you and your leaders "Gospelize *YOUR* Youth Ministry."

1. What were some specific factors that helped drive the explosive growth of the early church in the book of Acts?

2. What's one idea in this chapter that was new to you?

3. Do you agree with Greg's theory that Paul's disciple making strategy evolved? Why or why not?

4. How do you feel about the possibility of attracting "those" kinds of kids to our youth group?

5. What could we do to create an environment that is even more welcoming for newcomers?

6. Currently, what percentage of our students do you think would be able to disciple a new believer about the basics of the faith?

7. What are some specific examples of things we might start to do differently if we decided to be more intentional about nudging students forward in their spiritual growth?

8. Discuss the five-columned discipleship tracking tool. Would this kind of tool be helpful for our ministry? Why or why not? If so, discuss a plan for implementing this idea into your ministry.

9. Do you agree with Greg's assertion that one of the reasons most youth groups have fewer seniors than eighth graders is because we are not giving them a cause worth staying for?

10. Spend some time together praying for your ministry's disciple making and multiplying needs.

CONQUERING YOUR "14ER"

GOSPEL ADVANCING MINISTRY VALUE #5
A bold vision focuses it.

In Colorado, we call them "14ers." And there are 52 mountain peaks in Colorado that are over 14,000 feet high.

Conquering one of them is a big deal. Conquering all of them is a feat.

I'll never forget climbing my first 14er with my boy, Jeremy, who was 10 years old at the time. It was Grays Peak—one of the "easier" ones—located a few miles south of I-70 on the east side of the famed Eisenhower Tunnel. It extends 14,278 feet into the deep blue Colorado sky.

We got a late start—a no-no when climbing a 14er, so when we pulled up to the parking area close to the base of the mountain, it was already mostly full of cars. We were among the last people to attempt the climb that day.

The reason you want to get an early start climbing a 14er is because Colorado is notorious for afternoon mountain thunderstorms. Lightning kills an average of eleven people per year in Colorado—far higher than the national average—and many times these strikes happen to hikers on mountain peaks.[1]

Pulling into the parking lot, I was a bit shaken by how big the mountain appeared. I remember telling my son, "I don't know if we can do this, Jeremy. This mountain is way bigger than I thought."

Talk about a confidence builder.

But we decided to go for it anyway. And it was much harder than I had anticipated. The three mile or so hike to the base of the mountain was not too bad, but then the real trek began.

Step by step, we climbed the mountain. Bit by bit, our pace slowed down.

Soon after beginning the ascent, both of us got splitting headaches. This is normal when climbing mountains in Colorado. The deprivation of oxygen at high altitutdes can impact the body and the brain in weird ways—especially if you're not used to it. It can make you sluggish and nauseated. Although born and raised in Colorado, this was almost twice the elevation of where we live in the Denver area.

Above 8,000 feet, altitude sickness can occur, which in extreme cases, can lead to high altitude pulmonary edema (fluid in the lungs) or high altitude cerebral edema (fluid on the brain), both of which can be fatal. Suffice it to say that I kept an eye on my boy as we began that climb and started experiencing some of the milder symptoms of altitude sickness.

One of the most important things you can do when climbing a mountain is to hydrate. You want to drink water, water and more water three days leading up to your climb. You want to drink so much water that your urine is clear by the time you begin to climb—a fun fact provided at no extra charge. This ensures that your body is fully hydrated, which is especially important when climbing in the high and dry Rocky Mountains.

Halfway into the climb, our thighs and lungs were burning. We took several breaks along the way to catch our breath. Jeremy told me that he had started feeling sick to his stomach.

But we pressed on. We were determined to get to the top.

Three-quarters of the way up, we decided to count out 50 steps before we took a short rest. Eventually, that turned into 40 steps and rest, and finally, to 25 steps and rest.

At this point, Jeremy wanted to turn back. But we had come too far to quit.

By now, people who had already summited were walking past us in droves down this massive mountain, while we slogged up. All the while, I was keeping an eye on the skies for those sudden storms that could form in minutes in the wild weather patterns of the Mountain West.

Finally, heads pounding and bodies aching, the summit was within reach. We hurled ourselves toward the peak, using hands and feet to make our way up the last several yards.

I'll never forget the feeling of conquering this 14er so many hours after beginning the trek! I took my camera phone and did a 360 degree video of the mountain peak we had just scaled. Asking Jeremy how he felt summiting his first 14er, he answered with a single word before collapsing, "Nauseous."

By the time we got back to our 2002 Jeep Liberty seven plus hours later, we were exhilarated and exhausted. Jeremy's words to me at that moment are seared in my memory. "Dad," he said, "thanks for not letting me give up."

SPIRITUAL ALTITUDE SICKNESS

Giving up can happen in youth ministry just as easily as it does climbing a 14er. Except that in youth ministry, you can fake it. You can keep going through the motions, completing the latest flashy four-week curriculum and playing the latest music. And nobody but the Holy Spirit is the wiser that you have lost your enthusiastic "conquer-my-14er" attitude that launched you into youth ministry in the first place.

When many youth leaders first get into student ministry, they come in with aspirations for reaching every teenager in their community for Christ. They come in with hearts on fire and gospel guns ablazing. Their starry-eyed enthusiasm is innocent—some would say naïve—and intense. They are going to climb and conquer the 14er before them. Nothing will stop them…or so they think.

Then they go to a staff meeting where they're publicly berated for the stain on the carpet, because the horseplay got a bit out of hand last week. This triggers their first symptoms of SAS—Spiritual Altitude Sickness. Before long, their fast trek slows down, as they realize they are going to have to pace themselves.

But as the weeks give way to months, and the months to years, many grind their climb to a stop. They're tired of the headaches. They're nauseated by the politics.

So they begin to play the game instead of continuing the arduous climb to the peak of their original purpose in youth ministry. Five years later, if they survive that long, they've become the seasoned youth leader who knows how to run a youth program that is "good enough" to look effective.

Meanwhile, the community in which they serve remains largely unreached, their students are graduating with a shallow faith that shrivels up and blows away in the slightest breeze and the mountain they originally set out to climb remains unconquered.

STRIVING TOWARD A BOLD VISION

A bold vision is your personal ministry 14er. It's the mountain you want to climb when it comes to advancing the good news in and through your teenagers. Because prioritizing evangelism is often overlooked in the typical youth ministry, I'm going to very specifically zero in on what it looks like to build a vision that advances the gospel "through" your teenagers.

Let's start by taking a closer look at Jesus' charge to His followers in Matthew 28:

> Then the eleven disciples went to Galilee, to the mountain where Jesus had told them to go. When they saw him, they worshiped him; but some doubted.
>
> Then Jesus came to them and said, "All authority in heaven and on earth has been given to me. Therefore go and make disciples of all nations, baptizing them in the name of the Father and of the Son and of the Holy Spirit, and teaching them to obey everything I have commanded you. And surely I am with you always, to the very end of the age" (Matthew 28:16-20).

After His resurrection, Jesus told His disciples to meet Him back in Galilee on "the mountain." While nobody knows exactly which mountain He was referring to, if I were a betting man, I'd put my money on Mt. Arbel.

On my recent trip to Israel, I got to stand on its towering heights with 185 other ministry leaders, and listen to this passage exegeted by Bill Hodgson, an excellent Bible teacher from Australia. From

Mt. Arbel, you can scan the Sea of Galilee and see the general area where Jesus did most of His ministry.

When Jesus said those familiar words, *"teaching them to obey everything I have commanded you,"* the view from Mt. Arbel would have served as a kind of whiteboard, helping them remember the lessons Jesus had taught them. They would recall the lesson of faith when He calmed the water and the lesson of reaching the unreachable when they traveled to the pagan-filled "other side" of Galilee. From the beatitudes, to the challenge to "launch into the deep," all of these locations can be clearly seen from the heights of Mt. Arbel.

Whether or not this was the specific mountain, the disciples climbed some mountain in Galilee where Jesus was waiting for them. And on that mountain, He gave them another mountain to climb, bigger than Arbel, bigger than Grays Peak, even bigger than Mt. Everest.

It was the mountainous challenge to *"go and make disciples of all nations."* That word "nations" literally means "people groups." This means that the goal of every disciple of Jesus should be to make disciples, who make disciples, until every people group, tribe and nation has disciple multipliers who are reproducing disciples who can saturate their corner of the world with the message of hope.

Jesus rephrased this challenge in His last words to His disciples before He ascended into heaven. He told them in Acts 1:8: *"But you will receive power when the Holy Spirit comes on you; and you will be my witnesses in Jerusalem, and in all Judea and Samaria, and to the ends of the earth."*

JESUS' BOLD VISION

Actually, long before Jesus was the born on this earth, He was building a vision to advance His kingdom globally.

Go back 1,000 years before Christ was born, and you can see Him clarifying this vision through the pen of David as the psalmist wrote: *"All the ends of the earth will remember and turn to the Lord, and all the families of the nations will bow down before him"* (Psalm 22:27).

Go back 1,400 years before Christ, and you will see this vision taking shape as the Jews began to conquer the Promised Land when the author of Joshua declared: *"He did this so that all the peoples of the earth might know that the hand of the LORD is powerful and so that you might always fear the LORD your God"* (Joshua 4:24).

Go back 2,000 years before Jesus lived on earth, and you'll see God promising to bless the earth through Abraham's offspring (a.k.a. "Jesus"!) in Genesis 26:4: *I will make your descendants as numerous as the stars in the sky and will give them all these lands, and through your offspring all nations on earth will be blessed..."*

Go back to the account of the Fall, and you'll see God tipping His hand to the need for a Savior who will die in order restore what was broken and bring salvation to humanity: *"And I will put enmity between you and the woman, and between your offspring and hers; he will crush your head, and you will strike his heel"* (Genesis 3:15). The cross bruised the weight-bearing heels of Jesus, but crushed the sin-scheming head of Satan!

It was God's vision all along, even before the creation of the world to redeem a people as His own (Ephesians 1:4). And He will accomplish this vision. Revelation 5:9-10 make this crystal clear:

> *And they sang a new song, saying:*
> *"You are worthy to take the scroll*
>   *and to open its seals,*
> *because you were slain,*
>   *and with your blood you purchased for God*
>   *persons from every tribe and language and*
> *people and nation.*

You have made them to be a kingdom and priests to serve our God,
> *and they will reign on the earth."*

The question is not **if** His bold vision will be accomplished, but **will you be a partner with Him** in accomplishing it? If you allow the machinery of ministry and the downward pull of church politics to grind you down and wear you out, you may miss out on conquering that mountain at Jesus' side. He'll conquer it either way, but He wants you to go with Him.

Like my son, Jeremy, did with me after climbing that 14er, you will thank Him for not letting you give up in the painful pursuit of His bold vision.

POWER COMES THROUGH THE HOLY SPIRIT

Where do you find the power to climb this mountain and accomplish this shockingly large mission? Through the Holy Spirit who dwells within you! *"But you will receive power when the Holy Spirit comes on you…,"* Jesus promised in Acts 1:8. The Spirit is how you hydrate. He is your energy blast. He is the Third Person of the Trinity who dwells within you, to fuel you to accomplish THE Cause of Christ.

This is why it's vital you look at His power as an outlet, and not as a jumper cable. Too often, we have a jumper cable approach to our ministries. We go to church and get pumped up. We listen to that Matt Chandler podcast and get re-energized. We read our Bible in the mornings and think we're good.

But over the course of the day, we go from pumped up to drained out. And so we go in for another jumper cable jolt—Christian music, another sermon podcast, an encouraging talk with a friend—and we are good to go for another hour or two.

This is an exhausting way to live. Jumper cable Christianity goes from jolt to dolt, from cruising to crashing, from highs to lows.

But the steady current of the Holy Spirit dwells in you to give you the ongoing energy you need to accomplish His mission one step at a time. As you learn to live in a daily declaration of dependence on Him, you will have the energy you need to keep the pace so that you can conquer that 14er God has put in front of you.

Learning what it means to walk by the Spirit—and believe me, I'm still learning—is the most valuable lesson in my inner life. As I prayerfully depend on His power, instead of my own, He gives me the strength to conquer step by step by step. Sometimes I still get a headache over the ministry challenges along the way, and sometimes I'm even sick to my stomach. But He gives me the power to fight through these battles.

That's why I love the words of Paul in Colossians 1:28-29:

> So we tell others about Christ, warning everyone and teaching everyone with all the wisdom God has given us. We want to present them to God, perfect in their relationship to Christ. That's why I work and struggle so hard, depending on Christ's mighty power that works within me (NLT).

It's not easy. You still must *"work and struggle"* hard. But you can depend on Christ's mighty power through His Holy Spirit surging through your spiritual veins, as you seek to conquer this mountain.

STEP BY STEP BY STEP

The supernatural result of being filled with the Holy Spirit is to testify about Jesus. That's precisely what the Holy Spirit does, according to Jesus' own words in John 15:26-27:

> *"When the Advocate comes, whom I will send to you from the Father—the Spirit of truth who goes out from the Father—he will testify about me. And you also must testify, for you have been with me from the beginning."*

If you look closely at this passage, you can see the direct connection of the Holy Spirit testifying about Jesus and the disciples testifying about Him. The Greek word for the Holy Spirit, *paraclete*, means "advocate" or "counselor." *Meyer's New Testament Commentary* explains it like this:

> The Paraclete was to give testimony of Christ through the disciples, in speaking forth from them (Matthew 10:20; Mark 13:11). But the testimony of the disciples of Christ was at the same time also their own, since it expressed their own experiences with Christ from the beginning onwards, John 1:14; 1 John 1:1; Acts 1:21-22.[2]

The Holy Spirit was testifying about Jesus through the disciples. Nowhere is this more clearly seen than in Acts 2 when the Holy Spirit indwelt the believers, fulfilling what Jesus promised them in Acts 1:5. They began testifying in various languages, and a crowd gathered to listen to Peter's gospel explanation. As a result, 3,000 put their faith in Jesus on the spot (Acts 2:41).

The Spirit of God has been testifying about the Son of God through the people of God ever since. Our tongues are set on fire to testify about Jesus through the Spirit of God who dwells within us. When we resist that Holy Spirit urge to share the good news with those He has put in our path, we are quenching the Spirit and dousing the flame.

So what is the step by step plan Jesus gave us in this passage to bear witness to Him and His good news? Across the street, across the tracks and across the world!

"ACROSS THE STREET" (OTHERWISE KNOWN AS JERUSALEM AND JUDEA)

Jerusalem and Judea were the stomping ground of the early disciples, and represented their fellow countrymen, their neighbors, their friends and their families. Basically, Jesus is telling them to start where they are at and spread outward.

What applied to them applies to us. We, too, are to start by saturating our circle of friends, families, neighbors and others within our reach with the good news of Jesus. We are to pray for them with passion, pursue them with love and persuade them with the truth of the gospel.

My Jerusalem is called "Arvada."

Arvada is a northwestern suburb of Denver. Although I was raised in the city of Denver, I soon after moved to the Arvada area. This is where I planted a church, and where I've led Dare 2 Share from for the last quarter of a century or so.

When my lifelong friend, Rick Long, and I first planted Grace Church, I decided that I needed to map out my Jerusalem—the geographic area I was striving to saturate with the message of the gospel. So I charted out the main streets to the north, south, east and west of where our church was meeting at the time, and began to plot my strategy.

What was my "step by step plan" to conquer the mountain of Arvada with the gospel? It was going door to door, until I literally talked to everyone in the city about Jesus personally. If you look closely at the following map of my Jerusalem—which is still pasted into the front of my old preaching Bible—you'll see the lines demarking the streets that I walked down as I was going door to door.I was going to gospelize Arvada singlehandedly. Or so I thought. Over those months of door to door work, I developed an appreciation

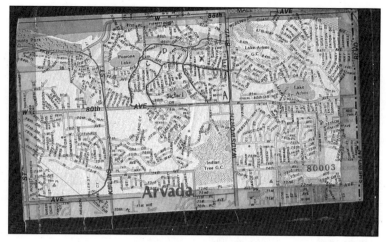

My map of "my Jerusalem."

for how hard it is for those young Mormon missionaries. Doors slammed in my face, dogs chase me away and curse words spewed in my general direction. One time I knocked on a door and began sharing the good news of Jesus when the lady interrupted me and said, "I'm a Jehovah's Witness." This struck me as funny, so I said, "And here I am on *your* doorstep!" And with that, I began to do a little Irish jig on her porch, while laughing hysterically. For some reason while this struck me as funny, she didn't share my opinion. So, SLAM!!!

Finally, it began to dawn on me that there was no way I could scale this mountain alone. I began to realize that if we could train and equip the people at our church to share the gospel within their own spheres of influence and mobilize *them* to make disciples who make disciples, then there was a possibility it could actually happen.

That's a big part of how the idea behind Dare 2 Share was born. I began to realize that to truly reach a city, people had to be mobilized for the cause of Christ to seek and save the lost. What was true in Arvada is also true in New York, Kansas City, Los Angeles, Houston and Lincoln, Nebraska.

It's true in your city, as well, which is your own personal "Jerusalem." My question to you is: have you identified the geographic area you are striving to reach for "THE Cause" of Christ—your ministry's "Cause Turf"? Have you prayerfully identified the streets north, south, east and west of your church within which you want every teenager engaged in a gospel conversation? You can start now, by prayerfully identifying your Cause Turf on the following grid.

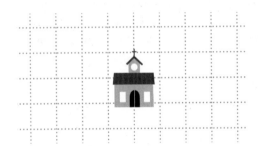

Draw the streets to the north, south, east, and west of your church that could represent the specific community God is calling you to reach...

As you consider the scope of your vision for advancing the gospel through your youth ministry efforts, I want to challenge you to be **bold.** A truly bold vision has to be so big that God has to show up in order for you to accomplish it. Your mountain should be so huge that you must recruit other like-minded youth leaders to join you.

Today, Grace Church is a congregation of 3,000+ members. I stepped out of Grace's pulpit several years ago, in order to move into full time ministry with Dare 2 Share, but my co-pastor and co-conspirator for THE Cause, Rick Long, has carried on the vision with excellence. He's even helped other churches in our city, and beyond, become more gospel advancing. Over 60%

of Grace Church's members came to Christ as a result of people within the church reaching their friends, neighbors, classmates and coworkers. They're still scaling the mountain, and are well on their way to the summit.

While being Jesus' witness in your Jerusalem and Judea is a great starting point, it doesn't stop there.

"ACROSS THE TRACKS" (YOUR SAMARIA)

In Jesus' time, the Samaritans were considered compromised half-breeds. Being half-Jew and half-Gentile was worse than being a pureblooded Gentile. That's why it was shocking to the Samaritan woman that Jesus would even acknowledge her presence, let alone ask her for a drink.

But it's often across the tracks where God does His best work. In Acts 1-7, the primary work of the disciples was in and around Jerusalem. But in Acts 8 a persecution, led by Saul and the Sanhedrin, broke out against the believers. Acts 8:1-5 describes it like this:

> ...On that day a great persecution broke out against the church in Jerusalem, and all except the apostles were scattered throughout Judea and Samaria. Godly men buried Stephen and mourned deeply for him. But Saul began to destroy the church. Going from house to house, he dragged off both men and women and put them in prison. Those who had been scattered preached the word wherever they went. Philip went down to a city in Samaria and proclaimed the Messiah there.

It took a great persecution to catapult the early church from just going "across the street," and into going "across the tracks." What happened as a result of Philip's preaching?

> When the crowds heard Philip and saw the signs he performed, they all paid close attention to what he said. For with shrieks,

impure spirits came out of many, and many who were paralyzed or lame were healed. So there was great joy in that city" (Acts 8:6-8).

And soon after:

But when they believed Philip as he proclaimed the good news of the kingdom of God and the name of Jesus Christ, they were baptized, both men and women (Acts 8:12).

 #GOSPELIZE *A truly bold vision has to be so big that God has to show up in order for you to accomplish it.*

I was raised on "the other side of the tracks." The area of North Denver I was brought up in had high crime and low income. But when Yankee crossed the boundary from the safety of suburban Arvada to the danger of the city in order to reach my family, everything changed for us.

Generally speaking, the poorer someone is, the more likelihood they will be open to the good news of Jesus. While I can't support this statistically, I think I can support it personally based on my own experience growing up in a poor family in a poor neighborhood. I believe Scripture also points toward this truth. Check these verses out:

> *"The Spirit of the Lord is on me,*
> *because he has anointed me*
> *to proclaim good news to the poor.*
> *He has sent me to proclaim freedom for the prisoners*
> *and recovery of sight for the blind,*
> *to set the oppressed free..."* (Luke 4:18).

> *"Blessed are the poor in spirit,*
> *for theirs is the kingdom of heaven" (Matthew 5:3).*

> *Then Jesus said to his disciples, "Truly I tell you, it is hard for*
> *someone who is rich to enter the kingdom of heaven. Again*
> *I tell you, it is easier for a camel to go through the eye of a*
> *needle than for someone who is rich to enter the kingdom of*
> *God"* (Matthew 19:23-24).

This doesn't mean that we shouldn't reach out to the rich. This simply means that, generally speaking, the poor—on the other side of the tracks—tend to be more open to the gospel. Charles Spurgeon recognized this in his preaching. His church ballooned to over 10,000—in an era when there were no sophisticated sound systems to amplify his sermons—and much of it was due to his reach into the gritty, economically underprivileged urban areas of London.

In his sermon, *Preaching for the Poor,* Spurgeon made the case that preaching to the poor is a very strategic ministry move. Here's how he put it:

> If we would fire a building, it is best to light it at the basement; so our Saviour, when he would save a world, and convert men of all classes, and all ranks, begins at the lowest rank, that the fire may burn upwards, knowing right well that what was received by the poor, will ultimately by his grace be received by the rich also.[3]

In the same way, as you identify your Cause Turf, I encourage you to put a highlighter on the apartment complexes, trailer courts and low income housing within it. If the area around your church doesn't have any of those, you may want to expand your Cause Turf further until it includes some! The teenagers in these areas may be grittier, but they may also be more open to the good news of Jesus than your typical suburban "rich" kid.

How does this principle translate to a Christian teenager on their school campus? They need to be encouraged to pray for, pursue and persuade not just the teenagers they are like, but also the ones they're not like. This may mean that at least one person in their Cause Circle is a broken, hurting, "poor in spirit" teenager—one of "those kids."

Of course across the tracks works both ways. Rich kids need Jesus too.

MULTICULTURAL YOUTH MINISTRY

Another aspect of reaching "into Samaria" that is crucially important is building a youth ministry that is truly multiethnic. The early church in Antioch was a powerful example of how God's plan was to build a multicolored, multicultured, multiethnic church that was full of Jews AND Gentiles.

This may not sound like a big deal to us, but at this period of history bringing circumcised Jews and uncircumcised Gentiles together in one church was a radical statement. As my friend Derwin L. Gray wrote:

> In all of human history, there has never been so much animosity, hatred, and violence between two groups of people as there has been between the Jew and the Gentile. But God birthed a group of people on the planet who He recreated in His eternal Son Jesus to transcend this racial hostility, injustice, and oppression. He did this by means of Jesus' death on the cross so that our hostility toward each other was put to death.[4]

As eloquent as Derwin is, the Apostle Paul puts it even better in Ephesians 2:11-18:

> *Don't forget that you Gentiles used to be outsiders. You were called "uncircumcised heathens" by the Jews, who were proud of*

their circumcision, even though it affected only their bodies and not their hearts. In those days you were living apart from Christ. You were excluded from citizenship among the people of Israel, and you did not know the covenant promises God had made to them. You lived in this world without God and without hope. But now you have been united with Christ Jesus. Once you were far away from God, but now you have been brought near to him through the blood of Christ.

For Christ himself has brought peace to us. He united Jews and Gentiles into one people when, in his own body on the cross, he broke down the wall of hostility that separated us. He did this by ending the system of law with its commandments and regulations. He made peace between Jews and Gentiles by creating in himself one new people from the two groups. Together as one body, Christ reconciled both groups to God by means of his death on the cross, and our hostility toward each other was put to death.

He brought this Good News of peace to you Gentiles who were far away from him, and peace to the Jews who were near. Now all of us can come to the Father through the same Holy Spirit because of what Christ has done for us" (NLT).

The church, yes, including your youth ministry, is to be a shining light of the racial unity that our connection with Jesus begins. Remember that old Sunday school song line that went, "Red and yellow, black and white, they are precious in His sight, Jesus loves the little children of the world"? It's true. He does!

But is that love that smashes racial boundaries reflected in the teenagers who attend your youth group, or is your group comprised of teenagers of just one race instead of being one body comprised of many races?

As I look back, one of the things that strikes me about the youth ministry I was reached by and raised in was the overwhelming number of teenagers who attended who were racially different from me. We especially had a high number of Latino teenagers who were involved in our ministry, many of them in key leadership positions in the youth ministry structure.

It didn't hit me much at the time, because nobody really talked about it. But looking back, I realize that there was an intentional strategy to make sure that every teenager in our community—and beyond—was reached with the gospel. Arvada, the city that this youth ministry resided in, was pretty pasty white at the time—and still is—so this high number of multiethnic teenagers were often bused in from the surrounding areas, including the city of Denver—where I lived.

That same reach-every-race DNA must have rubbed off on me as a pastor, because Grace Church, the church I pastored for 10 years, had a high percentage of families from multiethnic backgrounds. It still does.

As far as I remember, there was never a specific strategy to reach those of a different race. It was more "let's reach everyone across the street, across the tracks and around the world, no matter what race they are."

The gospel smashes boundaries—racial, socio-economic and the not-so-secret high school caste system of cool, uncool and in-the-middle kids. Your youth group should be a living, breathing example of the racial, cultural and social unity that only the church can provide through our co-unity with Christ!

"ACROSS THE WORLD" (TO THE ENDS OF THE EARTH)

We need to develop globally-minded teenagers who have a passion to reach the lost here, there and everywhere. That's one of the biggest benefits of gospel advancing missions trips. These ventures break the hearts of people around the globe.

GOSPEL ADVANCING STORIES FROM THE FRONT LINES
By Andy McGowan

It's so easy to get involved with ministry—the events and the daily grind—that we lose our focus while we do what we do. But establishing a bold vision will help you focus on the gospel of Jesus Christ, and help you make sure your ministry is advancing the kingdom of God.

When I came to my town, Kenosha, Wisconsin, I got together with a number of different pastors, and we started talking about how we could reach this city. But what we found out really quickly was that we got busy. We got busy with a lot of stuff that was actually preventing us from reaching the city with the gospel. And it took a tragedy for us to refocus.

A number of students in our community committed suicide, and it made us realize that the task at hand is much bigger than any of our own local communities, much bigger than any of our "know how," or our being a "professional" in youth ministry. What these suicides taught us is that we needed to get on our knees and pray, because the task at hand is much bigger than we are. And so that's exactly what we did. We got on our knees and we prayed, "God, we are desperate for you."

Together, as the pastors of the town, we were desperate to see our city turn around for Jesus Christ. And so we realized that it's not just our own church, but that it's through many churches coming together with the conviction of the gospel that we can take this city back for Jesus Christ.

So we began to meet together once a week. We prayed together, worshiped together, and as we led together, students began to follow, together in their schools. They began to reach their friends. Now some may say, "Well, wouldn't one church benefit if we all get together—like maybe the biggest church in town?" No, what we found was that when we led together with conviction and purpose, when we together focused on the gospel of Jesus Christ, then our students brought their friends to their own youth group. And our youth groups around town grew, because each youth group had a conviction that the gospel mattered. The gospel was our foundation.

I believe youth ministry is facing mission-drift when it comes to missions work. Far too many youth leaders view the "missionary" as an ancient relic of a bygone era who's thought of as little more than a dimly lit picture in the foyer of a steepled church on a *"Go ye into all the world"* missions wall. Missionaries are often ignored, marginalized or viewed as a necessity required to pacify the older tithers in the church and keep them happy.

Yet only a generation ago, missionaries were considered the risk-takers, revolutionaries and radicals in the church who would go into the highways and byways of foreign countries, risking life and limb for the sake of the gospel. That's a far cry from today, when they are often relegated to, at best, well-meaning but ineffective peddlers of Christianity, and, at worst, as an evangelistic brand of white colonialists trying to impose an American way of ministry on a not-so-receptive audience.

Sadly, in years past, this stereotype was deserved in some quadrants of missions work. Yes, there were—and in some cases, still are—those missionaries who've done harm to the name of Christ by preaching the right message in the wrong way (and sometimes the wrong message in the wrong way.) But these missionaries are the exceptions, rather than the rule.

Most of the mission organizations I've encountered over the years are much more culturally sensitive and strategic than many Christians realize. Effective missionaries have moved way past trying to do things the "old way," and are adapting and adopting the best practices of what it will take to reach a people group with the good news of Jesus.

Meanwhile, far too many youth leaders have intentionally or unintentionally de-emphasized missions work as an honorable and important vocation for their teenagers to pursue. For many, missions work has been replaced by social work, and evangelism has been replaced by humanitarianism. Instead of social justice serving as an enhancement for evangelistic efforts, it has become a complete replacement.

Ask on-fire Christian teenagers today what they want to do when they grow up, and you'll hear 10 different forms of humanitarian efforts, before you hear a single "I want to be a missionary."

The issues of human trafficking, social inequities and extreme poverty are close to the heart of God. Even a casual reading of Scripture makes it clear that issues of justice are key issues with God. Check these verses out:

> *He defends the cause of the fatherless and the widow, and loves the foreigner residing among you, giving them food and clothing* (Deuteronomy 10:18).

> *"Because the poor are plundered and the needy groan,*
> *I will now arise," says the Lord.*
> *"I will protect them from those who malign them"*
> (Psalm 12:5).

> *Defend the weak and the fatherless;*
> *uphold the cause of the poor and the oppressed.*
> *Rescue the weak and the needy;*
> *deliver them from the hand of the wicked* (Psalm 82:3-4).

> *Religion that God our Father accepts as pure and faultless is this: to look after orphans and widows in their distress and to keep oneself from being polluted by the world* (James 1:27).

Now listen, you rich people, weep and wail because of the misery that is coming on you. Your wealth has rotted, and moths have eaten your clothes. Your gold and silver are corroded. Their corrosion will testify against you and eat your flesh like fire. You have hoarded wealth in the last days. Look! The wages you failed to pay the workers who mowed your fields are crying out against you. The cries of the harvesters have reached the ears of the Lord Almighty (James 5:1-4).

It should be in our DNA to help the helpless, serve the broken and feed the hungry. Justice and Jesus go together.

And that's the problem. Too often they've been separated.

Yet the gospel message is at the root of the answer to every great humanitarian crisis on the planet. The poverty, trafficking and sickening of the human soul should be every believer's top priority, because it was Jesus' top priority (Luke 19:10). I love what the Assemblies of God denomination has done with their gospel advancing initiative called "The Human Right." Through this initiative, they are actively championing the truth that every human has the right to hear the gospel!

Of course, none of this negates our responsibility on a physical level to feed the poor, rescue the trafficked and help the sick. It actually deepens and sanctifies it. That's why over the last few hundred years, the greatest missions efforts have birthed the greatest humanitarian efforts. Why do you think so many hospitals start with an abbreviation for "Saint"—St. Anthony's, St. Joe's, St. Jude, St. Francis and so on? It's because these hospitals were birthed out of gospel advancing missions movements led by missionaries who sought to save the soul and heal the body.

But when the healing of the body eclipses the saving of the soul, it's a dark day indeed. That's one reason I'm convinced it's time to bring missions back to youth ministry. It's time to "re-heroize" missions work for the next generation. Let's make becoming a full time, gospel advancing missionary in an unreached people group a high calling again.

How do you do that? Here are some ideas:

- Take your teenagers on a short-term mission trip. Get them to feed the poor with bread AND the Bread of Life. Have them pass out water for the body AND Living Water for the soul. Get your teenagers to build houses for the poor on earth AND ones in heaven too.

- Share stories of missionaries, both past and present, who have and are powerfully advancing the good news of Jesus in other countries. Use Google and Bing as your allies to find stories and show videos that will inspire teenagers to have a global perspective when it comes to the good news of Jesus.

- Bring missionaries into your youth group to share stories and do a Q&A time with your teenagers so that they get a real sense of the power and impact of missions work. If your church is bringing in a missionary to speak in church, ask that same missionary to speak in youth group.

- Help teenagers gospelize their humanitarian aspirations. Whether it's stopping human trafficking or serving the poor, encourage your teenagers who feel genuinely called to humanitarian service to remember the importance of reaching the souls of those they serve with the hope that only Jesus can offer.

- Raise ongoing money to support missions.

- Do a yearly youth group series on global evangelism.

- Bring your teenagers out to Lead THE Cause. This week-long intensive is a crash course in evangelism, intercessory prayer and leadership training. In a very real sense, Lead THE Cause is a short-term urban missions week on steroids. And the teens who attend will get a heart for reaching the lost "across the street, across the tracks and around the world." At our last Lead THE Cause event fourteen teenagers committed themselves to full time overseas missions. We now have 14 more teenagers to conquer the 14er of global evangelism!

These are just a few ideas that can help you elevate the temperature of missions work with your teenagers and make Jesus-loving, gospel-advancing, people-serving missionaries heroes again!

DON'T GIVE UP!

Not long after our 14er expedition, I took my son Jeremy on a hike with one of his buddies. Jeremy was keeping pace, but his little buddy was straggling behind. It's not that the kid was out of shape, but he just didn't have the mental fortitude to finish the hike—even though we were only scaling one of the foothill and not a full-fledged, Colorado-sized mountain.

As we walked, I could hear them bantering back and forth. I heard his friend say, "Can we just stop? I'm getting tired. I want to quit."

To which my son said, "No. In our family, we don't give up."

I was beaming with daddy pride as we pressed on. Here was my son, who just weeks earlier was gasping for air and begging me to stop, embracing the benefits and blessings of refusing to quit.

In the same way, I challenge you not to give up. Prayerfully identify your own bold vision for your youth ministry, then keep pressing up that mountain.

We are all part of a heavenly family, a brotherhood and sisterhood of the redeemed. And in our family, we don't give up!

SPICE IT UP...

Questions to help you and your leaders "Gospelize *YOUR* Youth Ministry."

1. Did you identify with Greg's description of Spiritual Altitude Sickness?

2. Why is it helpful to have a "vision statement" for our youth ministry?

3. What makes a vision statement ***bold***?

4. Do we currently have a vision statement for our youth ministry?

5. If so, can everyone in our leadership group articulate what it is? Is it a good, bold vision statement? If not, do you think we should prayerfully craft one?

6. If appropriate, spend some time praying about a bold vision for your youth group.

7. Discuss the possible borders for your youth ministry's "Cause Turf."

8. Brainstorm some specific ideas for how your group could reach out "across the tracks."

9. Discuss some practical ideas for how you might begin to work in tandem with other youth ministries toward a common goal.

10. Discuss the list of ideas for "re-heroizing" missions work. Pick one that your group could try, and develop a plan for executing it.

COUNTING WHAT *REALLY* COUNTS

GOSPEL ADVANCING MINISTRY VALUE #6
Biblical outcomes measure it.

"Not everything that can be counted counts, and not everything that counts can be counted."

—William Bruce Cameron[1]

What are outcomes? They're what "comes out" of all our ministry efforts. Sadly, what comes out of far too many youth ministry efforts are apathetic teenagers with some memories the youth leader/"recreation director" managed to create sprinkled in along the way.

But down deep inside we all know what should be coming out of all of our youth ministry efforts, right? Teenagers who love Jesus with all of their hearts. Young people who know what they believe, why they believe, and are actively reaching their peers with the gospel. Graduating seniors who keep their faith long after the tassel is moved from left to right.

These outcomes are self-evident. They are what all of us are—or should be—aiming for in all of our youth ministry programming. Anything less is simply not a bold enough vision.

Throughout the book of Acts, you see several powerful outcomes that resulted from the apostles' Spirit-infused investment in the 1st century believers. Acts 11:19-23 provides a vivid example of multiple biblical outcomes:

> *Now those who had been scattered by the persecution that broke out when Stephen was killed traveled as far as Phoenicia, Cyprus and Antioch, spreading the word only among Jews. Some of them, however, men from Cyprus and Cyrene, went to Antioch and began to speak to Greeks also, telling them the good news about the Lord Jesus. The Lord's hand was with them, and a great number of people believed and turned to the Lord.*
>
> *News of this reached the church in Jerusalem, and they sent Barnabas to Antioch. When he arrived and saw what the grace of God had done, he was glad and encouraged them all to remain true to the Lord with all their hearts.*

In this passage, a handful of traveling preachers went rogue and traveled to Antioch to preach the gospel to the Greeks. This was a big deal, because up until then the disciples focused almost exclusively on reaching Jews and the relatively small number of Gentiles who had converted to Judaism (sometimes referred to as "God-fearing Gentiles"). But in this passage, these men from

Cyprus and Cyrene started sharing the gospel with straight up non-Jewish-in-every-way Greeks.

When the news of this unprecedented evangelistic activity among the Gentiles hit Jerusalem, the disciples there dispatched Barnabas, sending him 300 miles northward to Antioch to check things out. At this time, it appears that some Jewish believers were still a bit suspicious of Gentile converts to the faith. But when Barnabas came to Antioch and met with these Greek believers, he *"saw what the grace of God had done"* and *"was glad."*

What did he see? He saw outcomes in line with a great number of people trusting in Christ. Scripture doesn't tell us exactly what he witnessed. Perhaps he saw an evangelistic fervor that comes from being filled with the Holy Spirit—like the believers in Acts 4:31 who went out *"and spoke the word of God boldly."* Or maybe he witnessed a unity that could only be explained by the impact of the gospel—like the believers in Acts 4:32 who were *"one in heart and mind."* Or maybe he saw a selflessness that could only be explained by being transformed into a new creation through Christ—like the believers in Acts 2:45 who sold their possessions *"to give to anyone who had need."*

Whatever he saw, these outcomes were enough to convince Barnabas that these non-Jewish Greeks were now genuine 100% Grade A Christians. As a matter of fact, it's not the believers in Jerusalem who were first labeled "Christians" (a.k.a. "followers of Christ") by the unbelievers around them. According to Acts 11:26: *"The disciples were called Christians first at Antioch."* So we can conclude that the dramatic outcomes Barnabas saw were also clearly evident to the unbelievers in and around Antioch. These formerly pagan drinking buddies were now following the teachings of Christ both in creed and in deed.

"BARNABAS, MEET OUR YOUTH GROUP"

What evidence of biblical outcomes would Barnabas find if he visited your youth group? What kinds of outcomes characterize your teenagers' attitudes and actions that would convince Barnabas that they've experienced a true and deep encounter with Jesus?

Now, I'm not implying that your teenagers are not Christians—although some of them may not be. I understand that there can be Corinthian-type believers who are *"worldly—mere infants in Christ"* (1 Corinthians 3:1). But when Christians walk as non-Christians in their lifestyle choices, they do damage to the name of Jesus. So just like Paul lovingly confronted the Corinthians, we must lovingly confront truly believing teenagers and challenge them to align their lifestyle with their faith.

Again I ask the question. Are your teenagers living a life that is so definitively Christian that Barnabas would have no problem confirming their conversion by observing their transformed lives?

Just like the unbelievers nicknamed these Antioch-based believers "Christians," do the unbelievers at your teenagers' schools see enough evidence of the grace of God in the lives of your students that they could be nicknamed "followers of Christ"?

But Barnabas witnessed both qualitative and quantitative results. Not only did he see evidence of the grace of God in the quality of their transformed lives, he also saw evidence of the grace of God in the quantity of new disciples who were being added to the church. *"The Lord's hand was with them, and a great number of people believed and turned to the Lord"* (Acts 11:21).

Antioch was a picture of evangelistic health. It was a multicultural mix of converted Jews and Greeks—a model for the kind of the multicultural mix we should have represented in our churches and youth groups, by the way! And their growth was a direct result of disciples being made and multiplied.

If your youth group is growing, what is that growth attributable to? Is it transfer growth, because other Christian teenagers from other youth groups think you have a bigger, better program? Or is it new conversion growth, because your teenagers are personally engaging other teenagers with the good news of Jesus, and your youth group is a dynamic, seeker-friendly place where gospel conversations can coalesce and collide?

More on this later.

But first, I want to dive deeper into the topic of outcomes. I realize that many Christians tend to think that "measurable outcomes" sound too much like a secular business enterprise. But bear with me for awhile here, and I'll soon bring the conversation back around to youth ministry.

EVALUATING IMPACT

Consider the following classic "outcomes" diagram:

Input → Activities → Outputs → Outcomes → Ultimate Impact

Think of it like this…

> **Inputs** represent the time, energy and resources you invest in something.
> **Activities** represent what you do as a result of those inputs.
> **Outputs** are the immediate, short-term results of those activities.
> **Outcomes** are the long-term impact.
> **Ultimate Impact** represents the transformation that ultimately takes place in and around you as a result of those outcomes.

Let's use the illustration of working out as an example. Twenty years ago or so, I was completely out of shape. Although I was only 29 years of age, I walked with a pronounced limp—sadly, due to a dancing incident—and had ballooned to a non-muscle-bound 223 pounds. My low point was when my wife told me that I had my grandma's legs, and while I loved my pistol-toting grandma, this was definitely NOT a compliment.

Finally, my gym-rat, body-building, Jesus-loving buddy, Donnie, stepped in. "Enough is enough, fatty," he said. "You're going to the gym with me."

So the inputs began. I went to Better Bodies—though they should have called it "Butter Bodies" for me—where I gave them a down-payment and committed to the monthly fee. I also set time aside on my calendar to make working out a priority.

Soon after, I introduced even more inputs. I decided that in addition to working out, I would go in for a high-protein/low-carb diet. That meant I bought lots of beef and bologna.

Then came the activities. I had gym activities. I had kitchen activities. Donnie led the gym activities by helping me strengthen my severely atrophied right leg with a regimen of leg presses and squats. And I led the kitchen activities by disciplining myself to eat lots and lots of meat with no bread.

Soon the weight began to melt away. I went from 223 to 180 pounds in a matter of months. And that was the immediate output. I lost weight. But lost weight, while good, was not the outcome that I really wanted. Health is what I really wanted. And I was convinced that the high protein/low carb diet would not be a great long-term contribution to a healthy lifestyle.

So I began to focus more and more on eating healthy and imbedding exercise into my life. In the intervening years, while I've not been perfect, I've generally maintained this healthy lifestyle approach, and overall, I feel good and have avoided any major health problems. Because I work out and generally eat healthy, I have the energy I need to lead a ministry, run around the country training youth leaders and teenagers, write books and have a blast with my family.

My hope is that the ultimate impact of all this working out and healthy eating is a long and fruitful ministry, both personally and professionally. It's hard to advance the kingdom if you die prematurely due to a heart attack.

So how does this same principle apply in the world of youth ministry?

In the same way that I put time on my calendar for the gym and set aside money for beef in my grocery budget, your inputs are the time, manpower and resources you plan on investing in your youth ministry—think calendars, volunteers and budgets.

Like I spent time in the gym and invested the time it took to cook high protein food in the kitchen, your activities are the actual programs you're running. These may be small groups, youth group meetings, camps, conferences, outreach meetings and so on.

Like my fat beginning to melt away, these activities lead to your outputs. These will be things like the number of teens who attended, who indicated decisions, who joined a leadership team or a small group and so on.

Sadly, this is where many youth ministries stop. If I ask a youth leader, "How's it going?" They generally go straight to outputs, saying something like…

"It's great! We had 100 teenagers show up last week!"

"Things are pretty good. We had a great camp!"

"It's going alright. Our numbers were dropping for awhile, but it's leveled out."

But you must move on to outcomes. Like me becoming more and more physically healthy as a result of all my inputs, activities and outputs, the kinds of healthy outcomes you should be talking about are things like this…

> "Our growth has been steady, primarily due to teens reaching their friends for Christ."

> "We have ten more qualified student leaders actually leading the way for evangelism than we did last year at this time."

> "Our small groups have doubled because teenagers are bringing their friends every week and engaging in great spiritual conversations."

And what could be some of the "ultimate impacts" that you may see as a result of driving for these outcomes over a sustained period of time? Like me hopefully having a long and fruitful life, your youth ministry should see impacts like this…

> "Over the long haul, we're seeing that our graduating teenagers are committed to Jesus."

> "Our community is being transformed through the teen population being reached and revolutionized by their relationship with Christ."

RESULTS MATTER TO GOD

Now you may be thinking at this point, "That's all fine and good, but results are not my job. My job is to be faithful, and God produces the fruit. Didn't Paul say in 1 Corinthians 3:7 that some plant and some water, but only God makes things grow?"

But I would challenge you to consider the subtle underlying assumption of this mindset. It assumes that God may be reluctant to make things grow. When instead, He passionately wants to make things grow! As Jesus reminds us in Matthew 11:12: *"From the*

GOSPEL ADVANCING STORIES FROM THE FRONT LINES
By Carrie Evans

We all got into youth ministry because we wanted to make a difference in the lives of teens, right? And so, we ought to measure it to see if we're doing a very good job at that. It's important, because it will keep us motivated, focused and aligned with the plan of God if we are measuring the "right things."

It's so easy to get discouraged if we're just looking at things like who is showing up at our activities. So we need to step back and really think about some biblical ways to measure what it is that we are doing.

A couple of the things we look closely at in our group are the levels of sharing and serving. If you look at Acts 2, it explains that the believers had this deep sense of awe at the work of the Holy Spirit. And in response to that, they were willing to give everything that they had. So how is our group doing in comparison? Are they sharing and serving?

Obviously, we look at the number of salvation decisions that are being made, but another thing we look at as evidence of the Holy Spirit is how many of our teens are praying for or sharing a story about someone they are trying to reach with the gospel each week. What do those prayers and stories really tell us that can help us gauge their spiritual growth? Are they in awe of what God is doing?

Plus, we look at serving. Acts 2 says that the believers were willing to give everything that they had. How are our teens giving of their resources? Are they increasingly willing to give of their time, their talent, their resources and their money? Are they serving? Are they contributing in the name of Jesus to something outside of themselves in some way or another?

So measure. It gives you a pretty good pulse on how effective you're being if you can see an increasing level of sharing and serving.

days of John the Baptist until now, the kingdom of heaven has been forcefully advancing, and forceful men lay hold of it" (NIV, 1984).

God is pushing His kingdom forward and we—the *"forceful men"* in this verse—get to lay hold of it and push with Him! Like John the Baptist, we are working with God to push His kingdom ahead. This is the privilege God has given us—to join Him in His work!

He's actively working to make things go and grow. The real question is not whether or not He will make things grow, but whether or not you and I will be obedient enough for Him to use us to make things go!

Results are important to God.

At the end of the six days of creation, *"God saw all that he had made, and it was very good"* (Genesis 1:31a).

When He commanded Noah to build an ark, He didn't swing the hammer for Noah. Instead, He instructed him, empowered him and encouraged him.

When David stood before a nine foot six inch tall giant, God didn't swing the sling for him. But the Spirit of God infused him with courage to swing the sling, throw the stone and win the day.

When Jesus commanded His disciples to *"go and make disciples of all nations,"* He wasn't going to do the work and produce the results *for* them, but He promised to do the work and produce the results **through** them.

This dance between results and reliance is a tango between the divine and the human—which I'm not going to be able to totally explain in this short chapter, or ever for that matter!

As Francis Schaeffer, one of the premier Christian theologians and philosophers of the 20th century, said:

> In believing God's promises, we apply them...As we believe God for this moment, the Holy Spirit is not quenched. And

through his agency, the risen and glorified Christ, as the bridegroom of the bride, the vine, brings forth his fruit through us, at this moment. This is the practice of active passivity. And it is the only way anybody can live; there is no other way to live but moment by moment."[2]

The Christian life is an active process because we must "go." Jesus commanded us to *"go and bear fruit,"* and to *"go and make disciples."* But this is also a passive process, because only Jesus can *"bear fruit"* through us. Jesus reminds us in John 15:5: *"I am the vine; you are the branches. If you remain in me and I in you, you will bear much fruit; apart from me you can do nothing."*

FRUIT THAT WILL LAST

And what kind of fruit will Jesus produce in us when we stay connected to Him by faith and prayer? He tells us in John 15:16:

> *"You did not choose me, but I chose you and appointed you so that you might go and bear fruit—fruit that will last—and so that whatever you ask in my name the Father will give you."*

Consider that phrase, *"fruit that will last."* Now, think of it as the outcome and ultimate impact that Jesus will produce in you and through you, as you stay connected to Him and directed by Him!

Paul seconds this notion—not that Jesus needs his vote, but still... In 1 Corinthians 15:10 Paul says:

> *But by the grace of God I am what I am, and his grace to me was not without effect. No, I worked harder than all of them— yet not I, but the grace of God that was with me.*

Finding the sweet spot between God's grace *in* you and hard work *by* you is the key. As you proactively yield to Him, then He actively yields fruit through you. And He produces *"fruit that will last."*

This is the outcome you are seeking to generate as a result of all your youth ministry efforts, right? You want teenagers who keep their faith strong and vibrant. You want a youth ministry that is advancing the gospel in a way that will truly transform your community from the inside out. You want to look back at all of your youth ministry efforts someday and say, "It was worth it."

If "what gets measured, gets done," this means you must start measuring the right things.

As my friend Doug Holliday, the Executive Director of Sonlife North America, has pointed out, too many times preachers measure the three Bs: Budgets, Buildings and Butts in the seats. In the same way, a youth leader can easily be tempted to measure his or her success by how big their budget is, how cool their youth room is and how many teenagers are attending their weekly meetings.

But if these aren't the right things to measure, what is? We've already talked about some of the qualities that Barnabas measured with the church at Antioch. He measured their impact on both a qualitative and quantitative level. But let's dive deeper into these two areas of measurable outcomes when it comes to your youth ministry.

MEASURING OUTCOMES ON A QUALITATIVE LEVEL

How would you describe the quality of the teenager your youth ministry is producing spiritually? Do they know what they believe, and why they believe it? Do they have a "sticky faith" that will still be intact five months—or five years—from now? Are there spiritual maturation markers they are hitting?

Of course we need to guard against legalism here. Spiritual maturity is not a checklist of do's and don'ts. But there should be an upward spiral of spiritual growth that is demonstrated in the specific rhythms in their lives.

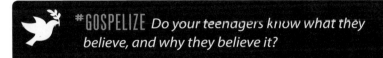

The writer of Hebrews gave a scathing review of how the scattered Jewish believers had been developing in their spiritual growth. The following passage makes it clear that they didn't have the outcomes that were expected of them given the amount of time they'd been believers:

> *You have been believers so long now that you ought to be teaching others. Instead, you need someone to teach you again the basic things about God's word. You are like babies who need milk and cannot eat solid food. For someone who lives on milk is still an infant and doesn't know how to do what is right. Solid food is for those who are mature, who through training have the skill to recognize the difference between right and wrong* (Hebrews 5:12-14, NLT).

From this passage, I believe there are at least four spiritual maturation markers that will help you define the quality of the teen disciples coming out of your youth ministry. Let's take a look at each.

Teaching Others God's Truth

"You have been believers so long now that you ought to be teaching others."

Whether it's in a one-on-one setting or in a group, spiritually maturing teenagers should be able to teach on some level. For example, at some point every Christian teenager in your group should be able to explain—or "teach"—the basic message of the gospel to others. Similarly, they should be able to explain what it means to be a Christian, how to pray and what it looks like to be growing in their relationship with Jesus.

I can't help but think back to my own youth group experience growing up. Our leaders taught us how to study the Bible, and how to teach it. As soon as possible, they had us teaching in Sunday school, youth group or some kind of Bible study. Soon eighteen-year-old teenagers were leading entire ministries and impacting tons of other teenagers in the process.

Some teenagers weren't excited about "public" teaching, so they did more of the one-to-one discipling of other teenagers. But all of us were expected to teach on some level, because there were so many new believers running around who needed grounding in the basics of walking with Jesus. And all the while, we ourselves were getting more and more grounded as a result of teaching others.

Wrestling with Deeper Theological Truths

"You are like babies who need milk and cannot eat solid food."

If you give a one-month-old baby a T-bone steak, it's not gonna go well. The baby is not going to be able to eat it. But if an eighteen-year-old is still using baby formula as his only source of nutrition, something is also radically wrong.

Your teenagers need to master the basics, and then learn to wrestle through deeper, meaty, theological truths. A good sign this wrestling has begun is when they begin to ask questions. That means the neurons in their brains are firing and the Spirit in their heart is stirring. You can help trigger spiritual growth by skillfully drawing out their questions and helping them find answers.

Growing Deeper and Stronger

"Solid food is for those who are mature, who through training have the skill..."

Teenagers who've hit this spiritual marker are building spiritual disciplines into their lives and actively seeking to live out their faith. Prayer, Bible study, Scripture memorization, silence and reflection become part of their spiritual rhythms. They are more than hearers of God's Word; they seek to be doers of it.

What percentage of your teenagers are actively reading their Bibles, praying and yielding themselves to God as a regular rhythm in their lives? How many even know how to do that? Have you taught your teenagers to pray? How to study the Bible devotionally? How to yield to the Spirit? Don't assume they know how. Start with the basics like any good coach and build from there.

Choosing Right from Wrong

"...have the skill to recognize the difference between right and wrong."

Do your teenagers have the ability to discern between right and wrong in the lyrics of a song, in the worldview of a movie or in the moral values of an app or game? Have they thought through and prayed through their playlist?

Teach your teenagers to sift through their playlist while imagining Jesus sitting right next to them. Ask them which songs they would keep, and which they would ditch if Jesus was right there. Then remind them that He is. Teach them to do the same thing with their movie and other media choices.

Of course there are other outcomes that can be measured, but Hebrews 5 gives you a good list to start with on a qualitative level. But what about on a quantitative level?

MEASURING OUTCOMES ON A QUANTITATIVE LEVEL

Let's revisit the following passage from Act 2:42-47. As you read it, watch for specific inputs, activities, outputs and outcomes:

They devoted themselves to the apostles' teaching and to fellowship, to the breaking of bread and to prayer. Everyone was filled with awe at the many wonders and signs performed by the apostles. All the believers were together and had everything in common. They sold property and possessions to give to anyone who had need. Every day they continued to meet together in the temple courts. They broke bread in their homes and ate together with glad and sincere hearts, praising God and enjoying the favor of all the people. And the Lord added to their number daily those who were being saved.

Did you spot the inputs and activities? They devoted themselves to teaching, fellowship, breaking of bread and prayer. Did you see the outputs? *"Everyone was filled with awe,"* and they met together *"with glad and sincere hearts."* Finally, did you notice the powerful outcome? *"And the Lord added to their number daily those who were being saved."*

Throughout the book of Acts—and much of church history, for that matter—one of the most powerful outcomes of a truly gospelized ministry is new believers. At Dare 2 Share, we refer to this as new conversion growth (NCG).

What percent of your teenagers have come to Christ as a direct result of your youth ministry? Is it 1%, 5%, 10% or more?

As I mentioned earlier, during the research project we commissioned a few years back, we found a core of youth leaders who actually attained a 25% NCG rate per year! That is phenomenal. But unfortunately, that is far from the norm. Christian author Dr. Dann Spader contends that 10% NCG is the minimum standard of evangelistic health.[3] By that standard, 25% is—in soccer speak—the winning gooooooaaaaaal in the championship game.

The vast majority of the teenagers at Youth Ranch—I'd estimate 80-90%—came to Christ as a direct result of its gospel advancing powerhouse of ministry efforts. The church I co-pastored for ten years has a 60%+ NCG. And it's because both of us co-pastors were part of the student leadership team at Youth Ranch when we were teenagers. We learned how to make disciples who make disciples there!

Why am I telling you all this? So that you know that all this talk of outputs and outcomes and ultimate impact is not conjecture for me. It's what I've learned and lived personally across the years, starting clear back in my pre-teen years!

And this lesson has also been personally and painfully further reinforced over the last few years of my ministry efforts at Dare 2 Share.

THE BOMB

"You mean we paid thousands of dollars to find out that we suck?" I yelled at our Executive Vice President.

I was fully expecting the research study we'd commissioned to support my premise that Dare 2 Share conferences lead to dramatic, transformative long-term outcomes and ultimate impact. For over two and a half decades, we'd been laboring under that assumption, and working our hearts out.

And we did discover that our conferences were super great at inspiring teenagers with unprecedented evangelistic passion. Immediately after attending our events, 76% of teenagers were sharing their faith. That was encouraging.

But the statistic that really discouraged me was that six months after the event, the percentage of teenagers who were sharing their faith dropped to 34%.

It felt like a bomb had blown up right over my head. I don't get depressed much, but for the next three days, I felt like quitting. I was as depressed as I've been in decades.

When I finally got our researcher, Jim Wert, on the phone, he talked me off the cliff. He assured me that, although there was a huge drop in evangelistic activity six months after the conference, 34% of a youth group sharing their faith is actually not too shabby. He also said, "This survey that you thought was going to be a marketing and fundraising tool is, instead, going to be a model shifter."

Jim then asked me what I thought the implications of the research were on a ministry level. My response was, "Well, obviously youth leaders aren't fully getting what we're trying to do. We're trying to help them make evangelism a year-round priority. We're trying to get them to drive the discipleship process by challenging their teenagers to risk everything and engage their peers with the gospel. Clearly, we've failed to give them enough training to make this happen."

And thus began the shift. We began to shift our focus as a ministry from primarily training teenagers to share their faith, to primarily equipping youth leaders to inspire, equip and unleash their teenagers year round to advance the gospel and make disciples.

While we're still in the midst of this switch, we have taken some huge strides in providing deeper, more robust training for youth leaders to lead the charge. This book is part of that switch. The week-long summer training event, Lead THE Cause, is part of that switch. Our Certified Trainer Program is part of that switch. The rallying of denominations and other para-church ministries to get behind the Gospel Advancing Ministry philosophy is part of that shift.

Why are we making the switch? Because to change our ultimate impact and outcomes, we have to change our inputs, activities and outputs! And now our bold vision for the ministry is crystal clear: "To mobilize 30,000 youth ministry leaders who will inspire and equip their young people to initiate gospel conversations with every teenager in America by 2025."

How will we measure it? Through the outcomes of these 30,000 Gospel Advancing Ministries—of which we are praying you will be one! By the way, if you haven't signed on to be part of the movement of youth ministries that are advancing the gospel, go to gospeladvancing.com right now, or download the free Gospel Advancing Ministry app on iTunes or Google Play.

Once you do, take the diagnostic assessment test. It will tell you whether you are "killing it," "making strides" or "need some work." And guess what? No matter what the results—good, bad or ugly—it won't cost you thousands of dollars!

Seriously, I'm grateful for that painful bomb that cost thousands of dollars that blew up over my head. From the shrapnel, God is building something better.

And that something starts with helping you gospelize your youth ministry and start to measure the things that matter.

It may be painful at first, but it's worth it!

SPICE IT UP...

Questions to help you and your leaders "Gospelize *YOUR* Youth Ministry."

1. Discuss the quote: "Not everything that can be counted counts, and not everything that counts can be counted."

2. Are you comfortable or uncomfortable with trying to measure the ultimate impact of our youth ministry efforts? Why?

3. What evidence of biblical outcomes would Barnabas find if he visited our youth group?

4. Do you agree that results are important to God? Why or why not?

5. Discuss Matthew 25:14-30. How does this parable relate to the outcomes that God expects of us?

6. Greg identified four spiritual maturation markers from Hebrews 5. How are the students in our group doing across those four milestones?

7. Walk through the ideas presented for measuring biblical outcomes in the "Gospel Advancing Stories from the Front Lines" feature. How is our group doing in each of these areas of sharing and serving?

8. What would you estimate our new conversion growth (NCG) rate to be?

9. Since "what gets measured, gets done," what are some biblical outcomes our group can begin to measure?

10. For a more comprehensive Gospel Advancing Ministry assessment tool, go to gospeladvancing.com and take the diagnostic assessment test.

CHAPTER 10

PROGRAM YOUR PRIORITIES

GOSPEL ADVANCING MINISTRY VALUE #7
Ongoing programs reflect it.

A few years ago, I met a hardworking ministry couple, Jason and Laura Loewen, who were serving as the youth leaders at Walloon Lake Community Church in Michigan. They'd met on a missions trip in South Africa, and the rest was history. They finished their time at Moody Bible Institute, got married and dove into youth ministry full time.

During their first few years of student ministry, it began to dawn on them that this youth leader role was a more-than-full-time job for both of them— even though Jason was the only one getting paid.

They took their teenagers to summer camps, winter camps, service projects and had monthly outreach meetings. In addition to that, they had their regular Sunday morning and Wednesday night youth meetings. Soon, they began to run themselves ragged, dashing from one youth event, to the next, to the next. They felt overcommitted and maxed out.

Sound familiar?

In their words, they had "far too much on their plates and were headed for burnout."

And, yes, their chaotic, chock-full list of activities also included bringing their students to Dare 2 Share conferences. But it was during one of these D2S youth leader training sessions, that Jason had a light bulb moment. I was talking about focusing on the priorities that mattered most, when Jason asked himself, "What if? What if we scratched the stuff that wasn't producing much fruit, and focused on a couple of things that had real potential for spiritual change in the lives of our teenagers?"

And that's exactly what Jason and Laura began to do. They streamlined. They cut. They put every event, program, outreach, camp, retreat and conference through a tight grid that asked the basic question, "How is this going to draw my kids closer to Jesus, and help them live on mission with the gospel?"

Laura wrote to us at D2S, and shared the impact this laser-like focus had yielded. Here's how she put it:

> By focusing more on the cross and equipping our teens…we've seen students, not only get saved, but be discipled long after the [D2S] conference was done. The adults at our church have all been incredibly challenged by our youth ministry, asking themselves: "If these teens can have a vibrant relationship with the Lord, and reach out to their friends, what the heck are we doing??"

For Jason and Laura, it wasn't just about bringing teenagers to a Dare 2 Share event, but about infusing a gospel advancing philosophy deep into the meat of their ministry. They began to intentionally drive these values into their youth ministry programming year round. And the result speaks for itself.

Several months after attending Lead THE Cause, the week-long summer intensive we now pull off in partnership with Sonlife, Jason wrote me:

> The eight students we took to Lead THE Cause became the backbone of our Wednesday night outreach program. They provided incredible leadership for our worship, greeting, games, teaching and Frontlines Ministry. (Frontlines is a student led, evangelistically-charged, weekly challenge.) At Lead THE Cause, we committed to pursuing 40% new conversion growth, which meant seeing 16 students give their lives to the Lord and become involved in the youth program. By Spring, we saw 20 students who gave their lives to the Lord and were getting involved in the youth ministry.

Soon after, this same DNA began to infect and impact the entire church as the senior pastor began to adopt and adapt these same values church-wide. But it all started with a hardworking youth ministry couple who were honest enough to say, "Enough is enough." It took a couple who were willing to risk everything to lead THE Cause of Christ and program their priorities into their weekly, monthly and annual calendar.

Sure, there have been battles, frustrations, failures and fallout. But the kingdom of God has been advancing in Walloon Lake, Michigan, because of this sold-out youth ministry couple who were willing to risk their old model, and try something different and dangerous. That "something" is a spicy new gospelized paradigm that's 2,000 years old.

That something can change the way you do youth ministry forever.

By the way, Jason and Laura were so effective at doing what they do, that we hired Jason to be Dare 2 Share's National Training Director. They now live in Denver, and are volunteering at a local church, helping to keep these values at the forefront of their church's youth ministry efforts.

MAKING YOUR CALENDAR WORK FOR YOU
By Andy McGowan

Do you own your calendar or does it own you? In the last decade of youth ministry, I have seen so many pastors burn out, miss opportunities and get involved with the wrong events and activities simply because they did not calendar their youth ministry with a gospel advancing purpose. I remember sitting down with a new youth pastor who was only in his third week in the ministry. He was overwhelmed as he stared at his blank calendar and the stack of conferences, camps, and training seminar fliers that lay on his desk. All too often, people say yes to an event without thinking of the bigger gospel advancing picture. When you set up a calendar, think of these three things.

1. Mission

When I first started youth ministry, I noticed there were a good handful of students that would show up for events, but not weekly youth group meetings. No youth worker likes seeing students become event junkies where there is no evidence of a Christian life beyond the weekend event. Whatever event, conference, or camp your ministry attends, you must look at the fruit that comes from each event and how the youth staff can shepherd and train in the aftermath. All too often, leaders send students to camps or Winter retreats with no vision of how to apply the teaching after the event. Don't choose events simply to entertain students and make your ministry look busy. Be strategic in how your event will motivate and equip students to live as followers of Jesus who share their faith in their everyday lives. As my friend Doug

Holliday says, "Discipleship begins and ends with evangelism." Do your research and say "yes" to what is gospel advancing, and "no" to what prevents you from being so.

2. Seasons

Events are a great way to anchor your students into your calendar year. Our student ministry calendar starts in September and ends in May. Instead of shutting down for the summer, we ramp up by having different themed nights and a training trip to Lead THE Cause. When choosing events or conferences, make sure you plan your event with the big picture in mind. Every event should flow into, instead of conspire against, each other. For example, as hundreds of unchurched students come to our church for our Fall outreach, we begin signups for our January Winter retreats. At our Winter retreats, we sign students up for our Spring training conference, and in the Spring we begin our big Summer missions push. Make no mistake, events are not discipleship, they are strategic moments for the ongoing discipleship and evangelism training that occurs in between. Your weekly message and your structure must reflect a gospel advancing mindset, lest you risk becoming an event driven ministry.

3. Connections

Continually tell your core students that the ministry calendar is not for them, but for their friends. In planning our outreaches, retreats, and even training events, we encourage our students to invite an unchurched friend. We ask adults—and even students—to donate half the ticket price for an unchurched friend's ticket. These friend tickets are a huge factor in helping us see so many outside students connect to a special event. Covering the price of a ticket shows we value advancing the gospel and that we value the person as our guest.

So how has your calendar been treating you? Is it adding value to your ministry? Are you seeing the kingdom increase, or is it sucking the life out of the momentum of what you could be? Go ahead and fill your calendar, but only with things that advance the kingdom. This will insure you will not be busy without a purpose…because nobody's got time for that.

PRIORITIZING THE ACTS 6 WAY

So how do **you** keep these gospel advancing values central to your programming? Let's go back, once again, to Acts 6:1-7, and look at it through a slightly different lens than we did in chapter 4. This time, let's dive deeply into this power passage in a way that can help transform the way you program your youth ministry going forward.

In those days when the number of disciples was increasing, the Hellenistic Jews among them complained against the Hebraic Jews because their widows were being overlooked in the daily distribution of food. So the Twelve gathered all the disciples together and said, "It would not be right for us to neglect the ministry of the word of God in order to wait on tables. Brothers and sisters, choose seven men from among you who are known to be full of the Spirit and wisdom. We will turn this responsibility over to them and will give our attention to prayer and the ministry of the word."

This proposal pleased the whole group. They chose Stephen, a man full of faith and of the Holy Spirit; also Philip, Procorus, Nicanor, Timon, Parmenas, and Nicolas from Antioch, a convert to Judaism. They presented these men to the apostles, who prayed and laid their hands on them.

So the word of God spread. The number of disciples in Jerusalem increased rapidly, and a large number of priests became obedient to the faith.

This passage clarifies three truths about programming your youth ministry:

1. Your priorities will always be reflected in your programs.
2. Your priorities can sometimes be complicated by genuine problems.
3. Your priorities must be constantly protected by laser-like focus.

Let's unpack each of these important truths.

1. Your priorities will always be reflected in your programs.

We will turn this responsibility over to them and will give our attention to prayer and the ministry of the word" (Acts 6:3b-4).

Taking care of the poor within the church was a priority for the early church, and their programs reflected it. But the leaders of the church—the apostles—had different priorities for the use of their time.

These apostles knew that their time was best spent on *"prayer and the ministry of the word."* Together through prayer they interceded on behalf of this fast-growing, mostly Jerusalem-based mega church. According to Acts 4:4, just the number of male converts was 5,000! In their ministry of God's Word, they taught theological truth to those who had become believers (Acts 2:42), and preached truth evangelistically to the unreached (Acts 5:41-42).

In this sense, they had an upward, inward and outward focus. They focused upward on God through prayer, inward on building up the believers through teaching and outward on reaching the lost through evangelism.

You can incorporate these same three priorities into your programming. There's something about putting each of these three priorities down on your program rundown—the order of "service" for your youth meeting—that solidifies them. Whether it's typed, scribbled or kept safe in your great big brain, this order of service reflects your list of priorities.

It's sort of like Billy Graham's familiar quote: "Give me five minutes with a person's checkbook, and I will tell you where their heart is."[1] In the same way, I can tell more about a youth leader's true priorities by what fills his/her rundown and ministry calendar than from any pithy mission statement on a wall or a website.

What do you have on your rundown sheet for this Wednesday night, or Sunday night, or whenever?

_____ Games? (Check!)
_____ Worship? (Check!)
_____ Fellowship time? (Check!)
_____ Announcements? (Check!)
_____ Teaching time? (Check!)
_____ What about intercessory prayer? (Hmmm...)
_____ What about evangelism? (Hmmm...)
_____ What about casting a bold vision? (Uh oh!)

If you want to begin to make prayer, discipleship and evangelism more and more of a priority in your ministry, start creating more and more time for it in your ongoing programs.

This is also true of calendaring your events. Whatever you put on your calendar, you prioritize. Maybe, like Jason and Laura, you have filled your calendar so full that you can't even tell what your true priorities are anymore.

It may be time to break out the scissors. It may be time to ask yourself "How is this event going to significantly draw my teenagers closer to Jesus and send them out to reach others?"

Here are a few questions to ask yourself before you put an event on your youth ministry calendar:

• Is this just another "fun" event with no deeper purpose?

• Will this camp really make an impact on my teenagers?

• Will this mission trip truly stretch my teenagers to not just serve the poor, but to share the good news of Jesus with them?

• How will this retreat prepare my teenagers to grow upwardly, inwardly and outwardly?

• Is this conference truly going to make a deep impact on my teenagers ongoing relationship with Jesus Christ?

- What transcendent purpose does this "all-nighter" have, beyond bonding us together as a group?

Of course, all of this talk of focusing doesn't mean that we refuse to have fun. Youth ministry is fun! And it should be fun! But there is **nothing** more fun than seeing a teenager being used by God to reach a peer with the message of Jesus. There is **nothing** more exciting than seeing a room full of teenagers praying and calling out to God on behalf of their unreached peers. There's **nothing** more thrilling than a teenage disciple making a disciple.

So the all-nighter, the mission trip and the retreat could—and maybe should—be put on the calendar, **if** you are willing to gospelize them!

Teenagers are busier today than ever with sports, games, friends, school, work and so on. So make sure whatever you do with them makes a maximum kingdom impact in them and through them.

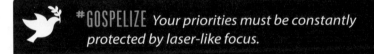

#GOSPELIZE *Your priorities must be constantly protected by laser-like focus.*

2. **Your priorities can sometimes be complicated by genuine problems.**

   In those days when the number of disciples was increasing, the Hellenistic Jews among them complained against the Hebraic Jews because their widows were being overlooked in the daily distribution of food" (Acts 6:1).

Okay, this was a genuine problem. There was a not-so-subtle form of favoritism playing out with those who led the food pantry of Jerusalem Community Church.

The Hellenistic Jewish widows, whose primary language was Greek, were looked down upon by the Hebraic widows, whose primary language was Hebrew. This looking-down-upon attitude soon turned into a back-of-the-line type situation, when it came to getting food.

This was wrong. There was a certain arrogance that often crept in among those who spoke Hebrew as their primary language toward the Jews who did not. They were prejudicially viewed as lesser citizens, because they spoke a "lesser" tongue.

This very real problem could have derailed the work of God in and through the early church in Jerusalem if the disciples had gotten distracted. But, instead of getting caught up in the minutia of trying to personally fix the problem by handing out the food themselves, they delegated the responsibility by saying: *"Brothers and sisters, choose seven men from among you who are known to be full of the Spirit and wisdom. We will turn this responsibility over to them"* (Acts 6:3).

The apostles didn't wait for the problem to go away. They didn't stop up their ears and sing a hymn. No, they recognized the very real problem, and let the people appoint a task force to fix it.

In the same way, there are real problems in youth ministry. We have youth rooms full of broken teenagers. Some may be addicted to drugs or porn, others may be cutters or suicidal, and most are wrestling through issues that range from identity to acceptance.

Some teenagers may need extra financial help due to a family situation or, in extreme circumstances, even a place to stay. Others may be failing or dropping out of school due to a learning disability or just plain apathy.

The more broken our society becomes, the more broken our teenagers become. But we can't lose sight of the fact that as youth leaders, we are responsible for *"prayer and the ministry of the word."*

We must help our ministries keep an upward, inward **and** outward focus. We can't focus solely on being educators, food providers and counselors, even though those needs may loom large.

Nor do we ignore the problem.

We prayerfully and carefully raise up other leaders in our midst to help us tackle these big challenges our teenagers are facing, and we authorize them to lead. We don't abdicate, we delegate. But we do it wisely, like the apostles did.

3. **Your priorities must be constantly protected by laser-like focus.**

    "It would not be right for us to neglect the ministry of the word of God in order to wait on tables" (Acts 6:3).

It's not right for you to forsake your upward, inward and outward priorities in order to set up the youth room. Not that you're above it. Not that sometimes we all have to do things someone else should be doing.

But you, as the leader, have the primary responsibility of keeping your youth ministry headed toward gospel advancement. Your "disciple ship" can easily get stuck in some random harbor. As the God-appointed captain of the ship, you must keep your eyes on Jesus Christ, your true North Star, and He will bring you to your gospel advancing destination.

Okay, that's literally all the seafaring analogies I can come up with—thank the Lord!

But my point is serious. You are the youth leader—the leader of youth—who must lead your students and adult volunteers toward gospel advancement, both in and through your students. You are the one who should drive these seven values deep into the heart of your youth ministry strategy.

GOSPEL ADVANCING STORIES FROM THE FRONT LINES
By Tyree Sterling

I used to think youth ministry was all about setting up chairs, tearing them down, programming—all these different kinds of things. I know you know it's so much more than just that stuff, but when you get frustrated, and you're in a rut, it tends to be what clouds your mind and becomes all that you seem to think about.

You see, I was trying to look at everybody else's websites, emails and podcasts, and I was trying to fit everybody else's stuff into my ministry.

So this value of "programming your priorities" was a total breath of fresh air to me. I was able to pray, and to find what is important to me for advancing the gospel in my youth ministry. I looked at my calendar. I looked at my weekly programming. I looked at the past, the present and the future events. And I've got to be honest, I was totally embarrassed. I was doing a lot of things on the calendar. I was doing a lot of things okay-ish, but I wasn't killing it in a couple areas of highest priority.

But now, I can honestly say that while before I was frustrated, now I feel like I'm alive again. I feel like I've started youth ministry all over again—like it's day one. So go through these gospel advancing youth ministry values, and God will begin to reveal to you whether this is a good idea or this is a God idea.

I'm a dreamer. I dream big. I can't stop thinking, and it's a great strength, but it's also a great weakness to me. But now I have a template of God ideas—of gospel advancing youth ministry ideas—to run crazy with.

So go ahead, pray, seek God, go through these gospel advancing youth ministry values. Go through the process, and see what God has for your specific youth ministry in your specific demographic.

SUGGESTIONS TO GOSPELIZE YOUR PROGRAMS

The gospeladvancing.com website and the Gospel Advancing Ministry app have tons more practical ideas—and I invite you to share your own ideas there, as well—so check them out. But I want to encourage you with three simple and very biblical ideas you can do right away. These suggestions will help you program some of these values into your regular meetings.

Idea #1: Give the gospel every week.

Why? Let me give you five reasons.

Giving the gospel every week...

1. **...subliminally equips your students to share the gospel themselves.**

    One of the reasons Christians don't share Jesus is because they don't know how. But when your students hear you explain the simple message of the gospel week after week, they are actually being trained to share the gospel themselves. Let me give you an example from my own experience.

    When I was pastoring Grace Church, one of our members approached me to tell me how he was sharing the gospel with a friend. I asked him where he had learned to explain the gospel. His response surprised and encouraged me. He said, "Greg, I've been hearing you give the gospel week after week after week in our church services. How could I not know how to explain the gospel after attending this church for years?"

2. **...creates "psychological agreement" with your teenagers.**

    When your students realize that sharing the message of Jesus is a non-negotiable for you, they are much more likely to bring their unreached classmates, teammates and friends to youth group. Many of them may not feel ready to share their faith yet, but they all can invite someone out to youth group, knowing that their friends will have an opportunity to hear the best news on the planet.

3. **...drives the power of its message deeper and deeper into the hearts of your Christian teenagers.**

Sometimes I hear youth leaders say they don't want to give the gospel every week because they don't want their teenagers to get sick of hearing it. What? We need to repeatedly hear the gospel, because we consistently forget the gospel! The book of Galatians is a re-preaching of the gospel to the Galatian believers. Romans is a re-preaching of the gospel to the Italian believers. In 1 Corinthians 2:2, Paul told the church in Corinth: *"For I decided that while I was with you I would forget everything except Jesus Christ, the one who was crucified."*

It never gets deeper than the gospel. It is the message that transforms us and our teenagers on every level, again and again and again. We need to share the good news with ourselves, our teenagers and all their unreached friends...relentlessly and repeatedly.

4. **...brings honor to Jesus.**

When we give the gospel, we are bringing glory to Christ in a very real way. If you think about it, the whole of Scripture centers around the person and work of Jesus. The Old Testament points to Him, the Gospels unveil Him, the Epistles explain Him and the book of Revelation exalts Him.

If the whole of Scripture centers around Christ and His cross, then shouldn't it be the "punch line" to every one of our talks? Every subject we touch on makes more sense in the shadow of the cross. Maybe that's why Spurgeon, when asked about his preaching style, said simply: "I take my text and make a beeline for the cross."[2] If you want to see Jesus honored, your students equipped and your community reached, take a cue from Spurgeon and make a beeline for the cross.

5. …was Jesus' idea.

With the installation of communion as a regular practice, Jesus insured that the message of the gospel would always be a top priority in the church. 1 Corinthians 11:26 reminds us that every time communion is taken, the gospel is given: *"For every time you eat this bread and drink this cup, you are announcing the Lord's death until he comes again."*

Based on Acts 20:7, it appears that the early church settled into a weekly practice of communion: *"On the first day of the week, we gathered with the local believers to share in the Lord's Supper."* This means that every week those who gathered together heard the good news of Jesus—believers and unbelievers alike.

We must let the gospel message bleed across everything. And because redemption is the theme of Scripture, *any* lesson can transition into the gospel. Working the gospel into your lesson application simply requires a salvation segue or transition statement. Here are a couple of examples of how this works:

- Self-Image Salvation Segue: One of the things that can really help people's self-image is when they find out that someone has sacrificed something for them. I know I definitely feel more valued when I find out someone has done something special for me that cost them a lot. Did you know that the God of the Universe made the ultimate sacrifice for you and for me? Here's how it happened…

- Anxiety Salvation Segue: It's easy to become fearful about the bad things that might happen to us. We could be diagnosed with a deadly disease, injured in a car accident or killed by a gunman on a shooting rampage. But an amazing thing I've discovered is that while I don't have a lot of control over what happens in this life, I do have a choice about what happens in the afterlife—and so do you. Here's how it works…

Each time you present the gospel, it's important to include an invitation to respond. Without providing students an opportunity to put their trust in Christ, it's almost like telling them they've just won a brand new car, describing it in detail, then not letting them in on how to claim their prize. When you share the gospel, you give students the greatest opportunity of their lives and they must be given a chance to take action. You can invite them to raise their hand, fill out a card or give some outward indication of their commitment so that you can follow up with new believers.

When you give the gospel weekly, both evangelism and discipleship are happening simultaneously! Jesus' message is being shared and you're discipling your Christian students by modeling how to bring the gospel up. As your teens hear your salvation segues each week, it will help them learn how to think about virtually every conversational topic as an opportunity to point people toward Jesus.

Idea #2: Create space for teenagers to share gospel advancing stories.

> *On their release, Peter and John went back to their own people and reported all that the chief priests and the elders had said to them. When they heard this, they raised their voices together in prayer to God* (Acts 4:23-24a).

> *On arriving there, they gathered the church together and reported all that God had done through them and how he had opened a door of faith to the Gentiles* (Acts 14:27).

> *When they came to Jerusalem, they were welcomed by the church and the apostles and elders, to whom they reported everything God had done through them* (Acts 15:4).

Why do we like the book of Acts? Because it creates a historical grid within which we can see the progression of the church and blah, blah, blah… NO! We love the book of Acts because of the stories in it! We are story-driven people, and the book of Acts tells us stories. We are like little kids on Uncle Luke's lap as he turns the pages and tells us story after story of transformed lives, persecutions and gospel advancement!

We need more stories in youth group, small groups and Sunday school—real life stories, from real life teenagers, sharing the real life gospel conversations they're having with their peers!

Some youth leaders call it "Take 5 for THE Cause," or "Pause for THE Cause," or simply "Open Mic," but whatever you call it, this is a time where teenagers can share stories—good, bad or ugly—about someone they are praying for, pursuing and/or persuading with Jesus' message of grace.

My friend, Kevin Bussema, who is National Director for Youth For Christ Core explains it like this:

> Stories are essential for developing young leaders, both as they grow in their personal walk with Christ and as they are mobilized for authentic Christ-sharing relationships with friends. Stories are a tangible, accessible way for Christian teenagers to talk about Jesus and connect with their friends. They become like viruses (in a good way!) that are easily caught and passed on. Sharing stories becomes less an evangelism method and more a way of living and creating connections to God in every relationship.

Teenagers shouldn't just share the exciting stories of radical conversions, but also the shut-me-down stories of getting dissed by their peers. Make this a time where teenagers can pray for each other, encourage each other and even coach each other.

Youth for Christ employs an excellent idea for this on their Core Teams. Every week believing teenagers meet to Share, Pray and Discover. They pray for each other and their lost friends. They learn something new from God's Word about living and sharing their faith. And they discover what they can do that week to nudge a friend, peer or classmate closer to faith in Jesus. Part of this is debriefing what happened last week and learning together how to become more effective at reaching their peers. Faith sharing becomes more of a rhythm that teenagers live out rather than just another curriculum they go through once a year.

Brilliant!

For more information about Core Teams check out www.yfc.net/core.

Gospel-centric storytelling also creates space for group learning. When teenagers know that sharing stories about sharing "The Story" is on the weekly agenda, it builds in accountability and the opportunity for teenagers to learn from each other. Together, they can learn to "fail forward," get ideas from each other and grow together as they pray for each other to be faithful in engaging others with the good news in the coming week.

There are a wide variety of creative ways to incorporate a story time into your group—open microphone, small group sharing, pre-taped videos of your teenagers sharing stories of gospel advancement, to name a few. Choose whatever fits your situation best. Just do something to make gospel advancing storytelling a priority!

Idea #3: Spend actual time praying for the lost in your meetings.

Again, I go back to 1 Timothy 2:1: *"I urge, then, first of all, that petitions, prayers, intercession and thanksgiving be made for all people."* Paul is instructing Timothy with the crucial reminder to program prayer first. We've already talked extensively about this in chapter 4, but prayer is so critically essential that it bears mentioning again.

The famous missionary Hudson Taylor once reported:

> Since the days of Pentecost, has the whole church ever put aside every other work and waited upon Him for ten days, that the

Spirit's power might be manifested? We give too much attention to method and machinery and resources, and too little to the source of power.[3]

Let's make room for the power of God in our programs, by making room for prayer in our programming.

A LIGHT BULB OR A LASER

A light bulb can brighten up a dark room. A laser can cut through steel.

Light bulbs disperse soft light in every direction for a short distance. Lasers can only be focused in a single direction, but theoretically, one beam can travel infinitely.

In the same way, your ministry is either a light bulb or a laser.

After His resurrection, Jesus gave His disciples a laser-like focus to *"go and make disciples of all nations..."* (Matthew 28:19). The book of Acts is the working out of this mission in real and tangible ways. The apostles relentlessly programmed their priorities in at every level. They delegated other pressing issues for qualified leaders to figure out, and kept gospel advancement—both internally, into the hearts of their people, and externally out into the world—absolutely central.

There are far too many nice, little 60 watt ministries that do nice, little 60 watt activities and get nice, little 60 watt results. These ministries shine some semblance of light, but usually it can't be seen outside the youth room they are meeting in on Wednesday nights. But laser-focused youth ministries have a single obsession. They love Jesus, and won't be satisfied until every teenager has encountered Him. They use their laser to cut out the lesser things from their programming and calendar.

Time to break out the laser.

SPICE IT UP...

Questions to help you and your leaders "Gospelize YOUR Youth Ministry."

1. Did you identify with the story of Jason and Laura feeling overcommitted and maxed out in their role as youth leaders?

2. Pray together, then jointly draft a statement that articulates your youth ministry's top priorities?

3. Are our ministry priorities being "complicated by genuine problems"? Discuss some possible strategies for addressing those genuine problems.

4. Talk through the youth group events that are currently on your calendar for the next three months, and ask the following question about each activity: "How is this going to draw our students closer to Jesus, and help them live on mission with the gospel?"

5. Brainstorm some things your ministry currently does that you could consider cutting out of your yearly program calendar.

6. Talk through your group's typical weekly rundown, using the following checklist:

   ___ Games?   ___ Teaching time?
   ___ Worship?   ___ Intercessory prayer?
   ___ Fellowship time? ___ Evangelism?
   ___ Announcements?   ___ Casting a bold vision?

7. Based on the checklist, how are you doing at programming your priorities?

8. Discuss the five reasons Greg provided when making a case for giving the gospel weekly. Do you agree with them?

9. Which of the three "Suggestions to Gospelize Your Programs" appealed to you the most? Why?

10. Brainstorm ways you could make room for one or more of the "Suggestions to Gospelize Your Programs" in your weekly program rundown.

CHAPTER 11

BEWARE THE PARTY POOPERS!

It was opening and I couldn't wait! Why? Because I love Boston Market, and it was the Grand Opening of a new store close to my house.

I strode in and ordered the half chicken and two sides, with a Diet Coke. The manager rang it up on the register and said, "That will be no charge, sir."

"What?" I asked. "What do you mean no charge?"

"Well," he explained, "since it's our Grand Opening, we're offering all food free today."

"It's free?" I asked, "Totally free?"

"Yes, sir," he responded.

"You're not kidding?" I shot back.

"No, sir," he said, starting to get a little frustrated with my disbelief. So he said it again. "All your food is free."

"Could I add a brownie onto my order?" I asked sheepishly.

"Of course, sir," he said with a smile.

"And it's free too?" I asked again.

"Completely," he assured me.

I was in heaven. Before me was a tray full of delicious Boston Market food—completely free.

As I sat down and began to dive into the steaming-hot chicken, mashed potatoes and corn on the cob, the food tasted especially delicious. I looked at the guy sitting across from me, and said one word between bites, "Free!" He nodded in agreement, and both of us chomped away on our completely free food.

By the time I devoured the brownie, and gulped down my last swig of Diet Coke, I was completely satisfied. Well, not completely. I had to get a refill of my pop before I left. And you guessed it—FREE!

Walking out to the parking lot with the large drink in hand, I saw some people headed in and said, "Did you know that all of their food is completely free today?" They looked shocked. "Free?" they asked. And I recounted the conversation I'd had with the manager. They rushed in to get their free food.

I got in my car, but decided that instead of just pulling out and going home, I would drive through the parking lot of the grocery store behind the Boston Market, and let the shoppers there know about the free food. Soon the line to Boston Market was long. Why? Because good news travels fast!

Like a crazy foodie fanatic, I drove up to various people pushing their shopping carts toward their cars or walking toward the store and yelled, "Hey! There's FREE food at Boston Market! Go and get some! FREE FOOD!" I scared a few people in the process, but I couldn't help myself. The food was free, and everyone had to know about it!

If I feel that way about Boston Market chicken, how much more excited should you and I be about the free gift of salvation? The Apostle Paul put it this way in Romans 3:22-24:

> We are made right with God by placing our faith in Jesus Christ. And this is true for everyone who believes, no matter who we are.

> For everyone has sinned; we all fall short of God's glorious standard. Yet God freely and graciously declares that we are righteous. He did this through Christ Jesus when he freed us from the penalty for our sins (NLT).

The good news is so good that we have to tell people! I saw this personally and powerfully when my family came to faith in Christ. They "drove through the parking lot," so to speak, to tell anyone and everyone the good news of Jesus. They told friends, coworkers, neighbors and strangers. They couldn't help themselves. They had tasted of grace, and they had to get that message out to everyone.

That's what we see happening in the early church between Acts 1 and Acts 14. The church exploded, spreading from Jerusalem to Samaria and beyond. Paul and Barnabas had gone on their first missionary journey, and their message was well received. Everyone everywhere was buzzing about the good news of this free gift of God through Jesus Christ.

CHIPPING AWAY AT THE MESSAGE OF GRACE

But then came the party poopers. No, not from outside the church, but from within.

> *While Paul and Barnabas were at Antioch of Syria, some men from Judea arrived and began to teach the believers: 'Unless you are circumcised as required by the law of Moses, you cannot be saved* (Acts 15:1, NLT).

The believers were used to attacks from the outside by unsaved Jewish leaders. But this attack came from believers within the church who had made the long trek to Antioch to pick a fight with Paul and Barnabas.

This attack brought their missionary movement to a complete halt. No longer could Paul and Barnabas just head out on another missionary journey. Instead, they had to take time out of their schedules to work this whole situation out.

In reality, these legalistic believers were keeping the gospel from spreading, because for the next several weeks at least, Paul and Barnabas had to deal with this situation by making the 300 mile trek to Jerusalem—and back—to meet with the apostles and address this.

What does this have to do with you and your youth ministry? As my old pastor used to say, "If Satan can't attack the messenger, he'll attack the message." In other words, if Satan can't destroy you personally through things like burnout, moral failure or a broken marriage, he will seek to attack your message. He knows that if he can get you preaching a lesser gospel, it won't spread as fast. He knows that if he can twist your message toward a works-based, pull-yourself-up-by-your-own-bootstraps theology, your gospel message won't be good news at all. It will be just another performance-driven message, from another performance-worshipping religion.

I've seen it in far too many youth ministries, and the scenario typically unfolds like the following real life example. A powerhouse youth leader was preaching the message of grace and advancing the good news in powerful ways in his city. His youth ministry was growing and thriving, and the gospel was making a big difference in his community.

But then the senior pastor started questioning whether these were "genuine conversions." Like the legalistic believers who attacked the message of Paul and Barnabas, this pastor chipped away at the grace message that was causing the youth group to thrive, and he sought to add conditions. He verbally attacked this youth leader's message as being incomplete. He made it clear that simple faith in Jesus wasn't enough, and that these teenagers had to go all in to serve Jesus, otherwise they couldn't be saved.

He tamped down the movement, and brought the grace party to a halt. The youth leader was shaken to his core by the confrontation, and by the trauma this legalistic party pooper inflicted on him and his youth ministry.

"OF COURSE WE'RE SAVED BY GRACE...BUT..."

The Christian legalists in Judea heard what was going on in and around Antioch. They heard that Gentiles were coming to faith in Christ in droves and these new converts were not at all like the many God-fearing Gentiles who had been willingly circumcised according to the law! No, these new Christians were straight up uncircumcised Gentiles. So the law-loving legalists decided to make a road trip, in order to educate these naïve believers that it just wasn't that easy. These Gentiles must be circumcised and keep the law—in addition to believing in Jesus, of course—if they truly wanted to be saved.

For these legalists, it was a matter of national pride that salvation came through the Jews. And if Gentiles could come straight to God as they were, then it felt like a slight against their Jewish heritage. No, the Gentiles must be circumcised, as well as keep the law, in order to be saved.

This was the first time this battle broke out in the early church, but it wasn't the last. The Galatian believers who had come to Christ through Paul's preaching were visited by some party poopers too. And the Galatian believers had bought the legalists pitch hook, line and sinker.

Paul writes his most scathing letter, not to the carnal believers of Corinth, but to the grace-forsaking believers in Galatia. Check out his emphatic protest in Galatians 1:6-7:

> I am shocked that you are turning away so soon from God, who called you to himself through the loving mercy of Christ. You are following a different way that pretends to be the Good News but is not the Good News at all. You are being fooled by those who deliberately twist the truth concerning Christ (NLT).

How can you identify these kinds of party poopers in your own church? Legalists are tricky creatures. They slither in the side doors of churches, sign up to lead Bible studies and fill the minds of once joyous believers with rules and requirements about what it "really" means to become a Christian. Ask them how a person is saved and they'll say, "By grace, of course." And then they'll roll out a scroll across the floor that's full of checklists to prove your salvation, complete with prerequisites you must abide by in order to receive this "free gift" of grace.

The Apostle Paul had strong words for the legalistic Judaizers of his time who wanted the Gentiles to accept God's grace through faith, but also be circumcised and keep the law of Moses, as well. Paul bluntly wrote about them in Galatians 5:12: *"As for those agitators, I wish they would go the whole way and emasculate themselves!"*

Wow.

Today, nobody—as far as I know—is seeking to add circumcision to the free gift of God's grace as a requirement for salvation. No, in our day, a far more subtle and sinister movement is creeping into the church. Twenty-first century Pharisees have replaced circumcision and keeping of the law with a more accepted "evangelicalized" list of do's and don'ts. These pious-sounding party poopers are causing Christians to doubt their salvation and land on the never ending treadmill of trying to prove, keep and/ or earn their salvation. These legalists are robbing believers of the joy that was once theirs in Christ and replacing it with the heavy yoke of legalism.

10 Ways to Spot a Legalist

How do you guard against the legalistic pressures of our day? You prayerfully keep your eyes peeled and your spirit attuned to anyone or anything that distorts Jesus' free grace! So with this in mind, here are 10 ways to spot a legalist:

1. They cheapen grace by focusing on what we must *do*, rather than on what Christ has *done.*
2. They'll say nonsensical things like, "Salvation is free, but it will cost you everything you have." (You can't have it both ways!)
3. They are "fruit inspectors," and hypothesize about how much spiritual fruit a person must produce in order to *truly* be saved.
4. They focus on things like turning, trying and crying, instead of on faith alone in Christ alone for salvation.
5. Their "gospel" could never be falsely accused of being a license to sin—like Paul's was in Romans 3:8!
6. They scare others with assertions that if you preach too much grace, people will run amok.
7. They conveniently avoid or mis-exegete large portions of gospel-centric New Testament books like Galatians, Romans and John.
8. They blend justification passages with sanctification passages, and then try to get us to drink a heresy smoothie.

9. They bake the same works-based righteousness cake that Mormons and Muslims do, but cover it with evangelical frosting.
10. They use the phrase "you mean to tell me…" a lot. Then they create worst case salvation scenarios about those who claim to be Christians, but abuse the grace of God. "You mean to tell me that someone can be saved and still…?"

But grace that cannot be abused is no grace at all. Grace that is not free is no grace at all. Grace that is not received by simple faith is no grace at all.

A generation ago, the famed Dr. Martin Lloyd Jones put it this way:

> The true preaching of the gospel of salvation by grace alone always leads to the possibility of this charge being brought against it. There is no better test as to whether a man is really preaching the New Testament gospel of salvation than this, that some people might misunderstand it and misinterpret it to mean that it really amounts to this, that because you are saved by grace alone it does not matter at all what you do; you can go on sinning as much as you like because it will redound all the more to the glory of grace. That is a very good test of gospel preaching. If my preaching and presentation of the gospel of salvation does not expose it to that misunderstanding, then it is not the gospel.[1]

Boom!

I like the way Paul put it in Romans 11:6: *"And if by grace, then it cannot be based on works; if it were, grace would no longer be grace."* It's either by grace, or by works. It can't be by both.

But here's the crazy thing about grace, once you receive it through faith, it begins to transform you. Jesus changes your "want-er," and you become a new creation. Sure we can abuse it, and, if we're honest, often do. But when we let grace do its work, it does exactly what the writer of Titus 2:12 describes: *"It teaches us to say 'No' to ungodliness and worldly passions, and to live self-controlled, upright and godly lives in this present age."*

God's grace is not a license to sin, but a reason to serve Jesus with reckless abandon—not because we have to, but because we get to.

If we resist, He persists. If we fail, He forgives. If we lose our faith, He remains faithful (2 Timothy 2:13). That makes me want to serve Him all the more. Sorry legalists, but grace is a better fuel.

As for you agitators, I wish you would go the whole way and...***cut it out.***

BE WILLING TO FIGHT FOR THE GOOD NEWS

"Paul and Barnabas disagreed with them, arguing vehemently" (Acts 15:2a, NLT).

There's a time to do battle. We want to be full of the Spirit as we stand for the truth, but be convinced of this, the Spirit is even more dedicated to the message of grace than we are. To keep our mouths shut is not an act of love. Because if we keep quiet, our teenagers will be shackled by the law, and the grace party will come to a screeching halt. Let me give you an example from my own life.

I knew something was up. Jerry (not his real name) wanted a meeting with me. He was part of a team of disgruntles who'd left the church I pastored in protest over something. He and his fellow crew of heavy metal musicians and "theologians"—seriously— decided to start their own ultra-conservative church. The message they were preaching reeked of works.

I went out to meet Jerry in the parking lot of Dare 2 Share's office. He was cordial, but cool. I asked him how one of his fellow musician/ theologian was doing, and he almost exploded. "I hate that guy!" he fumed. "He hurt me badly, and I will never forgive him!"

As we were walking inside, I counseled him that we must forgive as Jesus has forgiven us, like it says in Ephesians 4:32. No matter what this other band member had done to hurt him, it was nothing compared to what he and I—and all of us, for that matter—had done to Jesus with our sins. Jerry mumbled something under his breath, but it was clear that he wasn't going to forgive the other guy.

We settled into my office and I asked, "What's up, Jerry? What did you want to meet about?"

"I'm here to confront you on the false gospel that you are preaching!" He said this with the same bitter bile tone he had been spewing in the parking lot.

"What do you mean?" I asked, the hairs on my neck starting to rise.

"You preach easy-believism! You are making it too easy for people to be saved!" he said with an even louder voice.

"Really, Jerry? How easy is it to put my faith in a man I've never met (Jesus), to take me to a place I've never been (heaven)? It's so easy a child could do it. It's so hard that a religious person could choke on it," I shot back.

"No!" he yelled, his voice rising further. "A person has to turn from their sins and completely surrender their lives to Jesus to be saved!"

"Well, then," I responded, "I guess you're going straight to hell then!"

Now Jerry was mad, really mad. He bellowed, "What are you talking about?!"

"Jerry, you told me out in the parking lot that you refused to forgive your fellow musician for hurting you so badly. Your lack of forgiveness proves to me that you must not be saved!!"

He stood up and screamed, "Shut the $#!#% up!"

I shot back again, "Your foul language is proving you have an unregenerate soul!"

Now he was so mad that his fists were clenched. He looked like he was about to charge me. He yelled, "I'm gonna kick your @#$!"

"Sit down, Jerry," I said in a calm voice. "I'm just making my grace point here. If *you* can't even live up to the standards of the gospel you are preaching, how in the world could you expect someone who doesn't have the Spirit of God living within them yet to do so?"

He sat back down and we talked about the power of grace. Then he punched me. (Just kidding!)

When you preach the message of grace, the aggressive advocates of legalism will come at you like spider monkeys. Don't give into them for a moment. Have the hard discussions. Show them the way of grace.

THE WAY OF THE LAW IS IMPOSSIBLE!

But let's turn back to Barnabas and Paul. How did they handle this contentious situation? Acts 15:4-11 describes it this way:

> When they arrived in Jerusalem, Barnabas and Paul were welcomed by the whole church, including the apostles and elders. They reported everything God had done through them. But then some of the believers who belonged to the sect of the Pharisees stood up and insisted, "The Gentile converts must be circumcised and required to follow the law of Moses."
>
> So the apostles and elders met together to resolve this issue. At the meeting, after a long discussion, Peter stood and addressed them as follows: "Brothers, you all know that God chose me from among you some time ago to preach to the Gentiles so that they could hear the Good News and believe. God knows people's hearts, and he confirmed that he accepts Gentiles by giving them the Holy Spirit, just as he did to us. He made no distinction between us and them, for he cleansed their hearts through faith.

> *So why are you now challenging God by burdening the Gentile believers with a yoke that neither we nor our ancestors were able to bear? We believe that we are all saved the same way, by the undeserved grace of the Lord Jesus* (NLT).

Paul and Barnabas made their way to Jerusalem and gave a report of how the Gentiles had been radically saved—without being circumcised—and that's when some stood up and insisted: *"'The Gentiles must be circumcised and required to follow the law of Moses.'"*

How did Peter respond? First of all, it's important to note that they had *"a long discussion"* together. There was a genuine effort to come to a meeting of the minds. But Peter firmly, while relationally calling them *"brothers,"* reminded them that the way of the law is impossible when he asked: *"So why are you now challenging God by burdening the Gentile believers with a yoke that neither we nor our ancestors were able to bear?"*

If we go the way of the law, we have to go the whole way—perfectly, all of the time! That's what Jesus was communicating in the Sermon on the Mount. His list of *"You have heard…but I say"* points pierced the souls of those listening with the sheer impossibility of salvation through the law:

> *"You have heard that our ancestors were told, 'You must not murder. If you commit murder, you are subject to judgment.' But I say, if you are even angry with someone, you are subject to judgment!"* (Matthew 5:21-22a, NLT).

> *"You have heard the commandment that says, 'You must not commit adultery.' But I say, anyone who even looks at a woman with lust has already committed adultery with her in his heart"* (Matthew 5:27-28, NLT).

> *"You have heard the law that says, 'Love your neighbor' and hate your enemy. But I say, love your enemies! Pray for those who persecute you!"* (Matthew 5:43-44, NLT).

Then Jesus drops the punch line of the passage: *"But you are to be perfect, even as your Father in heaven is perfect"* (Matthew 5:48, NLT).

Imagine being in the crowd that day, listening to Jesus preach the Sermon on the Mount. By the time He was finished, everyone on the mountain knew that they deserved hell and were headed there. It was the most beautiful, horrific sermon ever preached.

Why did Jesus preach it? Because before we can really embrace grace, we need to be confronted by our sinfulness. And nothing does that like taking a long, hard look into the mirror of the law. That's what Paul was telling the Roman believers in Romans 3:20: *"Therefore no one will be declared righteous in God's sight by the works of the law; rather, through the law we become conscious of our sin."*

I am convinced this is also exactly what Jesus was doing with the rich young ruler in Mark 10. He was lifting up the mirror of the law to show him how sinful he really was. Let's take a closer look at this somewhat unsettling conversation.

THE RICH YOUNG RULER AND THE WAY OF GRACE

As Jesus started on his way, a man ran up to him and fell on his knees before him. "Good teacher," he asked, "what must I do to inherit eternal life?"

"Why do you call me good?" Jesus answered. "No one is good— except God alone. You know the commandments: 'You shall not murder, you shall not commit adultery, you shall not steal, you shall not give false testimony, you shall not defraud, honor your father and mother.'"

"Teacher," he declared, "all these I have kept since I was a boy."

Jesus looked at him and loved him. "One thing you lack," he said. "Go, sell everything you have and give to the poor, and you will have treasure in heaven. Then come, follow me."

At this the man's face fell. He went away sad, because he had great wealth (Mark 10:17-22).

There are certain passages that make us squirm, and this passage is one of them. You can't read the words of Jesus in these verses without thinking "Have I given up enough? Should I sell everything and give it to the poor? What does it really take to be saved?" We often leave this passage, like the rich young ruler, saddened, grieving and scratching our heads.

But was Jesus really saying that to get to heaven we have to keep The Ten Commandments and give all our stuff to the poor to be saved?

Now, I know you may be tempted to qualify this passage by thinking, "Well, no, but you have to be *willing* to do all of that?" But a mere "willingness" to give it all up robs this passage of its power. Jesus is asking the rich young ruler for more than willingness, He's asking him for everything.

If we are honest, in the deepest parts of our hearts, we know that we fall way short in the same way the rich young ruler did. We, like him, have broken the law—and according to Jesus in Matthew 5:21-30, we continue to break it every time we lust or hate. We all have something we've not given up—food, shelter, time, iPhone or whatever. We all fall short when it comes to following Jesus. And not only do we fall short, we fall grossly short, which Paul makes clear in Romans 3:23 when he declares: *"For all have sinned and fall short of the glory of God."*

I'm convinced that in this passage in Mark 10, Jesus was not painting a clear picture of the gospel for the rich young ruler. No, He was painting a clear picture of the law and the law's true requirements. In one brilliant stroke, Jesus helped this young man—who thought he was a pretty good person when he first approached Jesus—to see the covetousness, greed and narcissism that infected and motivated his darkened heart.

Maybe for the first time in his life, the rich young ruler understood that he was spiritually bankrupt before a holy God. Perhaps for the very first time he experienced a genuine and sobering conviction of sin.

It's interesting to me that Mark 10:21 tells us, *"Jesus looked at him and loved him."* Jesus so deeply loved this young man that He had to break him of his self-dependency and expose him for the sinner that he was. Jesus had to show him that, if he wanted to earn eternal life by keeping the law, he would have to go the whole way. It would take total obedience and full surrender all the time to every command for all of his life. Jesus had to show the young man the impossibility of trying to earn this brand of righteousness before God. Because it is only once people are convinced that they're sinners, that they know they need a Savior.

You see, the law is a mirror, not a washcloth. It can show us our sin, but it can't be used to scrub it away.

Jesus used the mirror of the law to showcase the utter depravity inside this young man's soul. Jesus used the letter and spirit of The Ten Commandments to help this ruler come to an awareness of the sin in his own life. Because it's only when a person understands that they are lost, that they can be found. So Jesus showed this young man that he was lost.

I wonder if in the frustrating years that followed this encounter with Jesus, whether or not God dispatched one of His followers to share the message of grace with this man whom Jesus loved. I can almost imagine that disciple sharing that this same Jesus who exposed this young man's sin so long ago, exposed His own back to the whip, exposed His head to a crown of thorns and His soul to God when He screamed, *"My God, my God, why have you forsaken me?"* This same judge who showed him how sinful he was, loved him enough to die in his place on the cross, so that through simple faith he could be saved.

Those who use this passage in Mark 10 to preach a you-better-give-up-everything-to-be-saved type of sermon are missing the deeper message of Jesus. Apart from Christ's death payment on the cross, we'll never be able to measure up to His standard of righteousness. We'll never be able to give up enough, sell enough or surrender enough—and that's the point.

That's the point of the law, the point of this passage and the point of this chapter.

 #GOSPELIZE *The law is a mirror, not a washcloth. It can show us our sin, but it can't be used to scrub it away.*

And once a person gets to the point in their life where they really understand this, he or she is finally ready to embrace the free gift of God's grace through faith in Jesus as their only hope of salvation.

Is the gospel you're communicating and equipping your students to share one that makes it hard to come to Christ (the way of the Law), or one that makes it easy (the way of grace)? Remember, that the Law is a *"yoke that neither we nor our ancestors were able to bear."* But grace is a party waiting to happen, good news ready to be told and a message ready to transform!

THE MILLION DOLLAR QUESTION

Several years ago, I ran into two gang members in the food court at the Citadel Mall in Colorado Springs. When I saw them, God moved in my heart to go up and initiate a conversation.

Both of these gang members were wearing the color red—they were members of the "Bloods"—and both of them were way bigger than me. One of the guys looked like he could have played linebacker for the Denver Broncos. And, interestingly, he was the only one interested in talking when the conversation turned toward Jesus.

He was riveted to every word I said. He was flexed and focused. When I explained the gospel, he was ready to respond. The end of the conversation went something like this…

"Does that make sense?"

"Yes," he responded.

"Then would you like to put your faith in Jesus right now to forgive you for all your sins, and receive the free gift of eternal life?" I asked.

"Yes," was his one word response.

Then I quizzed him to make sure he understood the gospel. "So if I see you 10 years from now, and ask you if you have eternal life, what are you going to say?"

He said, "Yes, I do."

"How do you know?" I asked.

"Because Jesus died for my sins and I trust in Him, not my good deeds to save me," was his spot-on response.

But I knew that God had placed me there in the middle of the food court as something more than a ticket puncher for a one-way trip to heaven. I knew that God had way more for this guy, because life with Jesus starts when we say "yes" to faith in Him, not after we die and go to heaven.

I wanted him to know the futility of the gangsta life, but I wanted to explain it in a way that would help him know that serving Jesus is a response that we have out of gratefulness, not guilt.

It was there that God gave me an illustration.

I asked him a hypothetical question, "What if I walked up to you and had a duffle bag full of cash. Let's say it contained one million dollars, and I came right up to you and offered it to you free of charge, with no strings attached. Would you take it?"

He thought for a second or two and said, "Yes, I would."

"After you took it, would you slap me in the face, push me to the ground, kick me and spit on me, and then walk away with the duffle bag?" I asked.

"No, I'd buy you a hamburger or something," was his hilarious response.

"Why would you do that?" I kept probing.

"Because I'd be grateful for the free gift," he responded.

Then I went in with the point of the entire fictional scenario, "Jesus just walked right into this food court, and through me, offered you something way more valuable than one million dollars. He gave you eternal life. He gave you hope. He gave you forgiveness of sins. Are you going to take His free gift, then spit in His face and walk away, or are you going to serve Him?"

"I'm gonna serve Him," he said with an expression of excitement.

"Why, because you have to, in order to be a Christian?" I asked.

"No, because I'm grateful for His free gift," he replied.

"What does this mean for your gang life?" I asked.

"It's over," he said bluntly.

In that one moment, in the middle of a food court, that gang member understood that serving Jesus is not something you have to do to earn, keep or prove your salvation. It's something you get to do out of sheer gratefulness for your salvation.

THE TRANSFORMATIONAL WAY OF GRACE!

Grace transforms. It transforms our teenagers from the inside out. If we don't see that transformation initially, we don't revert to preaching the law. Instead, we preach God's grace even more.

I love the words of Charles Spurgeon who said:

> When I thought that God was hard, I found it easy to sin. But when I found God so kind, so good, so overflowing with compassion, I smote upon my breast to think that I could have rebelled against One who loved me so and sought my good.[2]

The grace of God transforms us! We need to preach this message of God's grace again and again and again to our Christian teenagers so they walk in it, and to our unreached teens so they embrace it.

And when we do, the party is just getting started. Let's rush to the parking lot and tell everybody! Why?

It's free!!!!

SPICE IT UP...

Questions to help you and your leaders "Gospelize *YOUR* Youth Ministry."

1. Why aren't we more excited about sharing Jesus' message of grace?

2. Do you **really** believe that salvation is by faith alone in Christ alone?

3. What are some examples of the kinds of things 21st century evangelical Christians sometimes add to the prerequisites for salvation?

4. Of the "10 Ways to Spot a Legalist," are there any that you personally struggle with?

5. Discuss the following: "Grace that cannot be abused is no grace at all. Grace that is not free is no grace at all. Grace that is not received by simple faith is no grace at all."

6. Discuss the Greg's explanation of Jesus' conversation with the rich young ruler in Mark 10:17-22.

7. Do you have baggage from your past that sends you internal messages that chip away at the message of grace and say, "Of course we're saved by grace...**but**..."?

8. How do you think most of the students in our youth group would answer the Ten Million Dollar Question: "Are you going to take Jesus' free gift, then spit in His face and walk away, or are going to serve Him?"

9. Pair off and role-play explaining grace to someone.

10. Spend some time in prayer thanking Jesus for His free gift of grace.

CHAPTER 12

APOSTOLIC RESOLVE

I'm a sucker for the *Rocky* movies. There have been several times in my 25 years of marriage where my wife has happened to walk in during the end of one of the movies to catch me crying. That's right, crying. I realize I'm losing points on my man card by admitting that.

But what non-Rocky fans fail to realize is that the *Rocky* movies, especially the first one, are a love story and an endurance story. Boxing just happens to form the backdrop to the story for this boxing-on-the-side, over-the-hill, Italian leg breaker. But then, yo, love comes walking in, and her name is Adrian.

Rocky looks past the clunky glasses and the layers and layers of clothes to see the the girl of his dreams. For much of the movie he woos her, chases her and finally wins her over.

Out of the blue, through a crazy set of circumstances, he gets the opportunity to fight Apollo Creed, the heavyweight champion of the world. At first he turns it down, but finally gives in. Just before the fight, in a heart-to-heart talk with Adrian, he realizes that there's no way he can win the fight with Creed. He knows he's completely outmatched.

She asks him what he's going to do.

He thinks for a moment and says:

> "Who am I kiddin'? I ain't even in the guy's league...It don't matter, 'cause I was nobody before...I was nobody. That don't matter either, ya know...It really don't matter if I lose this fight. It really don't matter if this guy opens my head, either. 'Cause all I wanna do is go the distance. Nobody's ever gone the distance with Creed. And if I can go that distance, ya see, and that bell rings, ya know, and I'm still standin', I'm gonna know for the first time in my life, ya see, that I weren't just another bum from the neighborhood."[1]

At the end of the movie in the climactic scene, Rocky gets knocked down again and again, but he keeps getting up. And when the final bell rings, he's still standing. It's a split decision. The crowd goes wild. But instead of listening to the announcer letting everyone know who actually won the fight, Rocky starts screaming for Adrian. And Adrian comes running down the aisle, fighting her way up to the crowded ring—I'm tearing up even as I write this.

The movie ends with them holding each other in the ring, oblivious to the fact that he just lost. The movie ends with them exchanging the words, "I love you."

Fade to black...until the five sequels, anyway.

Rocky leaves me in tears every time, because that's how I want to live my life. I may not accomplish all my actual goals. I may fall short in many areas. But I want to fight in the power of Christ to the very end. And at the end of the final round of my life, I want to collapse into the arms of Christ and hear Him say, "I love you." He loves me, win or lose. He loves me, whether I accomplish my bold vision or not. And that makes me want to fight all the harder.

FIGHTING THE GOOD FIGHT

It was this same love that propelled the Apostle Paul to talk about having *"fought the good fight"* in 2 Timothy 4:7. Paul had "apostolic resolve," and he displayed it blow by blow in the ministry ring.

Aware that he was headed to Jerusalem, where he would begin to face a long series of innumerable hardships, he said goodbye to the beloved elders of Ephesus. Most of these brothers had most likely been trained by him at the School of Tyrannus, where he'd taught them to make disciples who make disciples. Acts 20:18-24 describes Paul's goodbye like this:

> When they arrived, he said to them: "You know how I lived the whole time I was with you, from the first day I came into the province of Asia. I served the Lord with great humility and with tears and in the midst of severe testing by the plots of my Jewish opponents. You know that I have not hesitated to preach anything that would be helpful to you but have taught you publicly and from house to house. I have declared to both Jews and Greeks that they must turn to God in repentance and have faith in our Lord Jesus.
>
> And now, compelled by the Spirit, I am going to Jerusalem, not knowing what will happen to me there. I only know that in every city the Holy Spirit warns me that prison and hardships

are facing me. However, I consider my life worth nothing to me; my only aim is to finish the race and complete the task the Lord Jesus has given me—the task of testifying to the good news of God's grace.

Paul's apostolic resolve shines through loud and clear. So let's unpack a few insights from this power passage that can help you stay rooted in Christ with this same brand of unshakeable determination, despite the inevitable trials that lay ahead.

1. Apostolic resolve is forged by humility, tears and testing.

In his farewell words, Paul addresses the hardships of ministry very specifically in verse 19, saying: *"I served the Lord with great humility and with tears and in the midst of severe testing by the plots of my Jewish opponents..."*

Quite honestly, most of us don't know what severe testing really is. Severe testing is what the modern-day Christians in Syria suffer as they are hunted down by Islamic extremists, just because they claim the name of Christ. Severe suffering is what the North Korean Christians experience locked away in prisons for years and tortured for having the audacity to put their faith in Jesus, instead of Kim Jong-un. Severe testing is what Paul endured again and again and again in his ministry that spanned three decades.

In 2 Corinthians 11:24-26, he runs through his litany of trials:

Five times I received from the Jews the forty lashes minus one. Three times I was beaten with rods, once I was pelted with stones, three times I was shipwrecked, I spent a night and a day in the open sea, I have been constantly on the move. I have been in danger from rivers, in danger from bandits, in danger from my fellow Jews, in danger from Gentiles; in danger in the city, in danger in the country, in danger at sea; and in danger from false believers.

How did God use all of this suffering in Paul's life? He used it to form and forge him into the image of His Son. He used it all to scrape away the self-dependence and make him super-dependent on Christ. In fact, in the very next chapter, Paul gives us "the secret" to his success...it was failure!

> *Therefore, in order to keep me from becoming conceited, I was given a thorn in my flesh, a messenger of Satan, to torment me. Three times I pleaded with the Lord to take it away from me. But he said to me, "My grace is sufficient for you, for my power is made perfect in weakness." Therefore I will boast all the more gladly about my weaknesses, so that Christ's power may rest on me. That is why, for Christ's sake, I delight in weaknesses, in insults, in hardships, in persecutions, in difficulties. For when I am weak, then I am strong* (2 Corinthians 12:7b-10).

What hardships are you going through right now? Maybe it's a budget hardship—personally or in your ministry. Or maybe it's a struggle with a fellow staff member who doesn't see eye-to-eye with you. It could be a secret battle with a lurid temptation, or a not-so-secret struggle with one of the leaders at your church regarding why youth ministry is still relevant.

In *Rocky Balboa*, the final movie in the *Rocky* series, a now senior citizen-aged Balboa has a talk with his adult-aged son, who is upset that his renewed fighting career might very well make him look bad. Rocky gives the best speech of his career on the streets of Philly:

> "Let me tell you something you already know. The world ain't all sunshine and rainbows. It's a very mean and nasty place, and I don't care how tough you are, it will beat you to your knees and keep you there permanently, if you let it. You, me, or nobody is gonna hit as hard as life. But it ain't about how hard you hit. It's about how hard you can get hit and keep moving forward; how much you can take and keep moving forward. That's how winning is done!

"Now, if you know what you're worth, then go out and get what you're worth. But you gotta be willing to take the hits, and not be pointing fingers saying you ain't where you wanna be because of him, or her, or anybody. Cowards do that and that ain't you. You're better than that!"[2]

Whatever the struggle, hardship, temptation or trial you are going through, don't give up. Keep moving forward in the power of Christ with humility and tears!

God wants to use those trials to make you super-dependent on Him. As you learn to trust in Him, He will forge you and form you into the image of His Son, the true Rock! He will make you fit for the bold vision He has put in your heart. Listen to these timeless words from Oswald Chambers about how our visions and our hardships collide in the valley:

> We always have visions before a thing is made real...God gives us the vision; then he takes us down to the valley to pound us into the shape of the vision. It is in the valley that so many of us faint and give way. Every vision will be made real if we have patience...God has to take us into the fires and floods to batter us into shape, until we get to the place where he can trust us with the veritable reality...Don't lose heart in the process.[3]

2. **Apostolic resolve is focused on preaching the truth, the whole truth and nothing but the truth.**

In Acts 20:20, Paul declares: *"You know that I have not hesitated to preach anything that would be helpful to you..."* Paul preached the whole counsel of God to the Ephesian believers. He gave them everything they needed to grow in their faith, and go with their faith to the ends of the earth. They grew both deep and wide— deep into the truths of God's Word and their relationship with Christ and wide into the world with the gospel—all based on the firm foundation of the death, burial and resurrection of Jesus. Paul's prayer for the Ephesians should be your prayer for your teenagers:

> *I pray that the eyes of your heart may be enlightened in order that you may know the hope to which he has called you, the riches of his glorious inheritance in his holy people, and his incomparably great power for us who believe. That power is the same as the mighty strength he exerted when he raised Christ from the dead and seated him at his right hand in the heavenly realms* (Ephesians 1:18-20).

Paul wanted these believers to realize they had an everlasting hope focused on the person of Christ, a glorious inheritance purchased by the blood of Christ and an unstoppable power made available through the resurrection of Christ.

As you seek to infuse the whole counsel of God into the souls of your teenagers, it will transform them from the inside out. It will give them ever increasing confidence to gospelize their peers, just like the Ephesians did in Acts 19:10 at the School of Tyrannus!

To do this, you must study the Word through the lens of the gospel, because it was written through that same lens. And you must preach it! You must challenge and equip your teenagers to dive deep into its riches, and you must unpack its life-transforming gospel advancing message week in and week out. As you do, your teenagers will become gospelized.

3.   Apostolic resolve is unflinchingly focused on completing the mission.

Paul was unflinchingly committed to completing the task Jesus had given him:

> *However, I consider my life worth nothing to me; my only aim is to finish the race and complete the task the Lord Jesus has*

given me—the task of testifying to the good news of God's grace (Acts 20:24).

God has given you a mission, your specific piece of advancing THE Cause of Christ in your own community. You must identify it, relentlessly pray over it and do everything you can in the power of Christ to accomplish it. There is a generation of teenagers in your midst who are literally on the highway to hell, and you and I have the message that can rescue them from it! Don't lose sight of this vital mission that God has placed firmly in your made-worthy-by-the-blood-of-Christ hands!

And be assured that your quest will have plenty of failures. You may fail again and again, but may you fail forward in the power of God.

#GOSPELIZE *Make the gospel central to everything you do, and you'll end up with a spicy dish people want to share with others.*

Have you ever heard the unofficial US Marine Corps' slogan "improvise, adapt and overcome"?[4]

As we've explored the book of Acts together across these 12 chapters, we've seen the church constantly doing just that. Again and again, they improvised, adapted and overcame. Their growth came through prayer, hardwork and duct tape.

These Spirit-fueled followers of Jesus started in the temple, but soon scattered to house churches. The Jerusalem apostles were quickly eclipsed by localized elders, as the church grew and expanded across Judea and beyond. When there were areas of service that needed to be taken care of, deacons were put in place so the leaders could focus on the ministry of the Word and prayer. When persecution hit the church in Jerusalem like a hurricane, the believers scattered and used it as an opportunity and preached the Word wherever they went. They would not be stopped.

When the Gentile believers came into the church of Antioch in droves, the legalists from Judea arose and pushed against this message of grace. But the church adjusted again. They clarified and codified the gospel message, corrected the legalists and re-sent missionaries out to make sure that everyone knew the true message of grace.

Along the way, letters were written and circulated from church to church—each one dealing with various areas of theology and practice. Between them, a canon of Scripture evolved containing the New Covenant in the form of 27 shockingly practical and powerful books.

Paul improvised, adapted and overcame, as well. When thrown in prison, he didn't sit idly by waiting for a better outcome. He wrote letters which were included in the canon. When he was forced out of the synagogue in Ephesus, he shifted locations to the School of Tyrannus, and he adjusted his strategy from addition to multiplication! There he unleashed an unstoppable force of disciple multiplication through the Ephesian believers.

The church was launched with an Acts 2 bang, and kept moving and adjusting and evolving until it had saturated much of the known world with the good news of Jesus. This unstoppable force, these blessed people, this community of love and truth, has been the ramrod in the hands of Christ for the last 2,000 years to batter the gates of hell and rescue souls headed to a dark eternity.

And now it's your turn to improvise, adapt and overcome. So take the seven values of a Gospel Advancing Ministry that we've been unpacking in this book, and find your own best recipe for building a gospelized youth ministry that fits your context. Make the gospel central to everything you do, and you'll end up with a spicy dish that gets people so excited they want to share it with others.

I end this book, not with the words of Rocky Balboa (Sorry, Rock), but with some of the last words of the Apostle Paul to his younger protégé, Timothy:

> *But you, keep your head in all situations, endure hardship, do the work of an evangelist, discharge all the duties of your ministry.*
>
> *For I am already being poured out like a drink offering, and the time for my departure is near. I have fought the good fight, I have finished the race, I have kept the faith. Now there is in store for me the crown of righteousness, which the Lord, the righteous Judge, will award to me on that day—and not only to me, but also to all who have longed for his appearing* (2 Timothy 4:5-8).

Let's fight the good fight. Let's finish the course! Let's keep the faith! That crown is waiting for you too.

So don't just stand there…

Gospelize!

SPICE IT UP...

Questions to help you and your leaders "Gospelize *YOUR* Youth Ministry."

1. How would you define "apostolic resolve" in your own words?

2. Do you have a personal hero—real or fictional—who has demonstrated unshakeable determination in the face of trials?

3. Have you ever faced severe suffering for the sake of your faith?

4. As a ministry, are we good at "improvising, adapting and overcoming"? What could we do to make us better in this area?

5. Spend some time praying about the challenges and difficulties your ministry is currently facing.

6. Pray Ephesians 1:18-20 over the students in your ministry.

7. What's the most impacting thing you learned personally from reading this book?

8. Would it be a good idea for some of us to ask our senior pastor to read this book, and then to meet with us to talk about it?

9. What do you think our ministry's top three "take-aways" should be as a result of reading this book?

10. Together, brainstorm an initial plan for implementing those "take-aways."

END NOTES

Chapter 1

[1] Spurgeon, Charles Haddon, Sermon 114: "Preaching for the Poor," *Spurgeon's Sermons Volume 03:1857* (Grand Rapids, MI: Christian Classics Ethereal Library, Public Domain), 81.

[2] Moore, Lecrae, "After the Music Stops," (Atlanta: Reach Records, 2006).

Chapter 2

[1] Maclaren, Alexander, *Expositions of Holy Scripture: The Acts* (Grand Rapids, MI: Christian Classics Ethereal Library, Public Domain), 11.

[2] Barker, Kenneth, *The NIV Study Bible* (Grand Rapids, MI.: Zondervan Bible, 1985), 1721.

[3] Timothy Keller, tweet on @timkellernyc, July 29, 2013.

Chapter 3

[1] Gaffigan, Jim, "Bottled Water" *Comedy Central: Stand-Up*, Episode 306, Posted 07/12/2000, cc.com/video-clips/pymif1/stand-up-jim-gaffigan--bottled-water.

[2] Goodreads, "Goodreads.com," *Robert Frost Quotes*, goodreads.com/author/quotes/7715.Robert_Frost.

Chapter 4

[1] Allen, Thomas; Berry, F.; Polmar, Norman, *War in the Gulf* (Nashville: Turner Publishing Company, 1991), 147.

[2] Spader, Dann, *4 Chair Discipling* (Chicago: Moody Publishers, 2014), 26.

[3] Bounds, E.M., *Power Through Prayer* (Grand Rapids, MI: Zondervan Publishing House, 1962), 12.

Chapter 5

[1] Green, Michael, *Evangelism in the Early Church* (Grand Rapids, MI: Wm. B Eerdmans Publishing Co., 2004), 321.

[2] Mercer, Tom, *8 to 15, The World Is Smaller Than You Think* (Oikos Books, 2013), *Kindle* digital file.

[3] Knight, Shawn, "Survey: The average teenager has more than 425 Facebook friends." Techspot.com, http://www.techspot.com/news/52665-survey-the-average-teenager-has-more-than-425-facebook-friends.html, May 22, 2013.

[4] Thayer, Joseph Henry, Carl Ludwig Wilibald Grimm, and Christian Gottlob Wilke, *Thayer's Greek-English Lexicon of the New Testament: Coded with the Numbering System from Strong's Exhaustive Concordance of the Bible* (Peabody, MA: Hendrickson, 1996), 497.

[5] Hirsch, Alan, *The Forgotten Ways* (Grand Rapids, MI: Brazos Books, 2006), 57.

[6] Spurgeon, Charles, *Lectures to My Students* (Lynchburg, VA: Old-Time Gospel Hour, 1875), 36.

Chapter 6

[1] Goodreads, "Goodreads.com," *A. W. Tozer Quotes*, goodreads.com/author/quotes/1082290.A_W_Tozer.

[2] Ray Vander Laan, "Rabbi and Talmidim," That The World May Know Ministries, Holland, MI, thattheworldmayknow.com/rabbi-and-talmidim.

[3] Gladwell, Malcolm, *The Tipping Point* (Boston: Little, Brown and Company, 2006), *Kindle* digital file.

[4] "Minority Rules: Scientists Discover Tipping Point for the Spread of Ideas," *RPI News*, Rensselaer, July 25, 2011, http://news.rpi.edu/update.do?artcenterkey=2902.

[5] Quotes, "Quotes.net," *Howard Hendricks Quotes*, quotes.net/quote/48425.

Chapter 7

[1] Keathley, J. Hampton, "The Commendation and Thanksgiving (1 Thess. 1:2-10)," *1 Thessalonians: An Exegetical and Devotional Commentary*, published February 2, 2009, bible.org/seriespage/commendation-and-thanksgiving-1-thess-12-10#P449_88402.

[2] Ray Vander Laan, "Province of Asia Minor," That The World May Know Ministries, Holland, MI, thattheworldmayknow.com/province-of-asia-minor.

[3] Bock, Darrell L., *Acts* (Grand Rapids, MI: Baker Academic, 2007), 601.

[4] Spader, Dann, 4 *Chair Discipling* (Chicago: Moody Publishers, 2014), 103.

Chapter 8

[1] Rocky Mountain Hiking Trails.com, "Lightning and what you can do while hiking," rockymountainhikingtrails.com/lightning-hiking-rocky-mountains.htm.

[2] Meyer, Heinrich, *Heinrich August Wilhelm Meyer's NT Commentary Critical and Exegetical* (Edinburgh: T. & T. CLARK, 1880), translated from the sixth edition of the German by Rev. Peter Christie, translation revised and edited by Frederick Crombie, D.D., John 15:26-27, digital version.

[3] Spurgeon, Charles Haddon, Sermon 114: "Preaching for the Poor," *Spurgeon's Sermons Volume 03:1857* (Grand Rapids, MI: Christian Classics Ethereal Library, Public Domain), 75.

[4] Gray, Derwin L., "#Ferguson: Why We Need More Multi-Ethnic Churches," ChristianPost.com, CP Opinion, August 15, 2014, m.christianpost.com/news/ferguson-why-we-need-more-multi-ethnic-churches-124895/.

Chapter 9

[1] Cameron, William Bruce Cameron, "Informal Sociology: A Casual Introduction to Sociological Thinking," 1963, 13.

[2] Schaeffer, Francis, *True Spirituality* (Carol Stream, IL: Tyndale House Publishers, Inc, 1971 [2012 edition]), 77.

[3] Spader, Dann, 4 *Chair Discipling* (Chicago: Moody Publishers, 2014), 103.

Chapter 10

[1] Think Exist, "Thinkexist.com," *Billy Graham Quotes*, thinkexist. com/quotation/give_me_five_minutes_with_a_person-s_ checkbook/332189.html.

[2] Drummond, Lewis A., "The Secrets of Spurgeon's Preaching," Christian History and Biography, *Christianity Today*, January 1, 1991, ctlibrary.com/ch/1991/issue29/2914.html.

[3] Taylor, J. Hudson, "The Source of Power for Christian Missions," *The Missionary Review of the World, v. LIII* (New York: Missionary Review Publishing Co., Inc., 1930), p. 516.

Chapter 11

[1] Lloyd-Jones, Martin, *Romans: The New Man, An Exposition of Chapter 6* (Grand Rapids, MI: Zondervan, 1973), 8-9.

[2] Spurgeon, Charles, "Repentance after Conversion," Sermon 2419, June 12, 1887.

Chapter 12

[1] *Rocky* (Santa Monica, CA: MGM Home Entertainment, [2014], originally released 1976).

[2] *Rocky Balboa* (Culver City, CA: Twentieth Century Fox home Entertainment, 2014).

[3] Chambers, Oswald, "Vision and Reality," *My Utmost for His Highest Daily Devotionals*, http://utmost.org/classic/vision-and-reality-classic/.

[4] Santamaria, Jason A., Vincent Martino, and Eric K. Clemons, *The Marine Corps Way: Using Maneuver Warfare to Lead a Winning Organization* (New York: McGraw-Hill, 2004), 149.

ABOUT THE AUTHOR

 Greg Stier is founder and CEO of Dare 2 Share Ministries, a ministry that has equipped over a million teenagers and adults to relationally and relentlessly share the gospel of Christ.

As a former church planter and pastor, Greg believes in the power and potential of the church to transform entire cities with the gospel. As a former youth leader, he is committed to seeing this transformation erupt from the next generation. Greg is the author of seventeen books and countless articles. He has appeared on CNN, CBN, TBN, Focus on the Family and several radio programs. He is a regular contributor to *Christian Post*, Churchleaders.com and *Group Magazine*. He has been a featured speaker at Promise Keepers, Youth Specialties, Creation Festival, LifeFest and The Billy Graham Schools of Evangelism. Greg has been married to Debbie for twenty-five years. They have two children whom he adores and one dog which he tolerates. Greg resides with his family in Arvada, Colorado.

OTHER BOOKS BY THIS AUTHOR

Firing Jesus

Dare 2 Share: A Field Guide to Sharing Your Faith

Life in 6 Words

*Outbreak: Creating a Contagious Youth Ministry
through Viral Evangelism*

Firestarter: Fuel Your Passion

Ministry Mutiny

Co-Authored Books

Youth Ministry in the 21st Century: Five Views

For more information visit

dare2share.org and gospeladvancing.com.